Victims of the Environment

*Loss from Natural Hazards in the
United States, 1970–1980*

Victims of the Environment

Loss from Natural Hazards in the
United States, 1970–1980

Peter H. Rossi
James D. Wright
Eleanor Weber-Burdin
and
Joseph Pereira

Social and Demographic Research Institute
University of Massachusetts
Amherst, Massachusetts

PLENUM PRESS • NEW YORK AND LONDON

Library of Congress Cataloging in Publication Data

Main entry under title:

Victims of the environment.

Bibliography: p.
Includes index.
1. Disaster relief—United States—History. 2. Disaster relief—United States—Research—United States. 3. Natural disasters—Economic aspects—United States. 4. Natural disasters—Social aspects—United States. 5. Social surveys—United States. I. Rossi, Peter Henry, 1921–
HV555.U6V52 1983   363.3'48'0973   83-19228
ISBN 0-306-41413-9

© 1983 Plenum Press, New York
A Division of Plenum Publishing Corporation
233 Spring Street, New York, N.Y. 10013

Printed in the United States of America

Preface

The research reported in this volume was designed to provide estimates of the extent of damages and injuries from certain natural hazards inflicted on households in the United States. In addition, it reports on sources of aid proffered to households and the extent to which there are differences among households in the receipt of help.

This volume represents the latest installment in a series of monographs stemming from the Social and Demographic Research Institute's (SADRI) program of research on the effects of natural hazard events in the United States. The first volume in our series (Wright, Rossi, Wright, & Weber-Burdin, 1979) reported on the long-range effects of natural hazards on the population and housing stocks of neighborhoods and communities. The second volume (Rossi et al., 1982) assessed the support for hazard mitigation policies existing among local and state political elites in a sample of states and local communities in the United States. The main findings of these two monographs can be summarized as follows. First, long-range effects (up to 10 years postevent) of natural hazard events are minimal: Local communities and neighborhoods that have been impacted by floods, tornadoes, or hurricanes appear to be no different in their population and housing growth patterns over the period 1960 to 1970 than comparable communities that went unscathed. Apparently, household and community resources plus outside aid were sufficient ordinarily to restore impacted areas to normal growth patterns. Second, our study of political elites indicated that few were deeply concerned about the risks of natural events or showed strong support for measures

v

such as zoning regulation designed to lower the occupancy of high-risk areas.

The issues of natural hazards risks and hazard mitigation measures paled in comparison to issues that involved immediate material interests, such as inflation and unemployment. Indeed, it appeared as if the only local and state elite members that were deeply concerned with hazard mitigation issues were those whose professional roles required that they be concerned with such issues. Accordingly, Civil Defense and American Red Cross officials, for example, were among those most in favor of their states and local communities adopting hazard mitigation policies and those most knowledgeable about alternative policies.

The results of these first two studies were discussed in some detail at a conference held in 1980 in Washington, D.C., attended mainly by social scientists concerned with the socioeconomic aspects of natural hazard impacts. The papers given at that conference along with summaries of the ensuing discussions are published in Wright et al. (1981).

One of the conclusions of the conference was that the socioeconomic effects of hazards were only partially measured at the level of neighborhoods within local communities. An appropriate next step in the documenting of the unsettling effects of natural hazards would be to study their impact on the more fine-grained level of households. Because, in the ordinary natural-hazard event, few households would be directly affected, the effects of such events ordinarily would be swamped and hence could not be detected on the neighborhood or community levels.

Accordingly, we designed the research described in this volume to reach a large sample of households and to locate those that had directly experienced the impact of floods, tornadoes, hurricanes, and earthquakes over the 11-year period 1970 through 1980.

The research reported in this volume was generously supported by the National Science Foundation under Grant #PFR-7926741. William Anderson of the National Science Foundation (NSF) staff monitored the grant and provided advice and encouragement over the two years involved. We were helped by many individuals. Fred Bates of the University of Georgia, Richard Berk of the University of California at Santa Barbara, Charles Fritz (formerly of the National Academy of Science/National Research Council), Ugo Morelli of the Federal Emergency Management Administration, William Petak of the University of Southern California, Roy Popkin of the American National Red Cross, and William Anderson of the NSF formed an advisory committee that provided help in the design of the study and offered helpful criticisms of the drafts of the instruments used. Gilbert White of the University of Colorado provided a critical review of an early draft of the manuscript. Of course, neither the National Science Foundation nor the advisory committee should be held responsible for the faults of the study reported or for its implications.

Audits and Surveys, Inc., of New York City collected the data reported in this volume under subcontract to the University of Massachusetts. Of course, the instruments used were designed by the SADRI staff, with Audits and Surveys organizing and carrying out the two-stage household survey involved.

As usual, we have been blessed with a secretarial staff— Jeanne Reinle, Ken Forfia, and Cindy Coffman—whose patience in dealing with the research staff is only exceeded by the skills they bring to the task of making our sprawling drafts into readable documents.

Peter H. Rossi
James D. Wright
Eleanor Weber-Burdin
Joseph Pereira

Contents

ix

List of Tables

Chapter 1

Chapter 3

Chapter 6

Appendix A

Natural Hazards Victimization

An Overview

Existing estimates of the total annual losses from all natural hazards vary from $5 billion to $10 billion, counting all costs—direct and indirect, public and private. Although the variation from estimate to estimate is very large, all agree that the annual toll is in the billions. Such estimates typically are constructed by summing across various component costs, some of which may be very precisely known (e.g., Small Business Administration—SBA—disaster loans) and some of which may be charitably regarded as "educated guesses" (e.g., local community expenditures). Perhaps the least well known among the components are the costs that are borne by victimized households, for which no centralized records are maintained by either federal agencies or national private relief organizations.

The main purpose of the research reported here is to provide more precise and all-encompassing estimates of the damage and injury tolls experienced by *households* and arising out of natural hazards. The approach taken was to survey by telephone a large national sample, chosen randomly, of approximately 13,000 telephone-owning households and to locate those who recalled experiencing a flood, a hurricane, a tornado, or an earthquake during the period 1970 through 1980. To provide a comparative frame, experiences with household fires were also studied. A subsample

1

of the 2,600 households that claimed one or more hazard experiences was contacted by mail with a questionnaire asking for detailed information on injuries, damages, financial and other aid received, and contacts with disaster agencies. Approximately 1,400 questionnaires were returned.

The research design employed allowed the screening of large numbers of households in order to reach the small proportion that had been victimized by natural disasters. Using "random-digit-dialing" sampling methods, it is possible to reach a random sample of telephone-owning households relatively inexpensively. Mail surveys ordinarily suffer from relatively low response rates, but they are also efficient and cost-effective in reaching households spread throughout the United States. The details of the designs used and the response rates are discussed in great detail in Chapters 2 and 3, where it is shown that the biases introduced by nonresponse are small.

Recent research on data collection methods indicates that telephone and mail surveys produce data that are indistinguishable in quality from those generated by face-to-face interviews (Groves and Kahn, 1978; Dillman, 1978). Furthermore, if one follows appropriate procedures, response rates can be obtained that are high enough to bolster the generalizability of the data obtained through telephone and mail surveys. These issues are discussed in detail in Chapter 3.

THE INCIDENCE OF DISASTER EXPERIENCES

The mass-screening telephone survey can also be used to estimate the incidence and distribution of hazard experiences (see Chapter 4). In terms of the least stringent definition of hazard experiences—self definitions of "experiencing" such an event, regardless of whether injuries or damages resulted—about 1 in 4 households experienced at least one such hazard event per decade, amounting to an annual projected number of about 4 million affected households.

The above definition includes any experience, including clearly trivial events that caused neither injuries nor damages to the households in question. In terms of a more stringent definition of nontrivial events or *victimizations* that includes only those hazard experiences causing injuries and/or damages, the incidence is lowered to about 25 per 1,000 households annually or, if we omit household fires, to about 19 per 1,000 households. Table 1.1 contains estimates of annual victimization rates for each of the hazards.

Slightly more than half of the annual hazard victimizations involve tornadoes or severe windstorms that happen to nearly 800,000 households each year. About equal in incidence are

TABLE 1.1
*Annual Rates of Natural Hazard Victimizations[a] and Projected
Annual Numbers of Households Affected*

| | Natural hazard victimization[c] | |
Hazard	Annual rate per 1,000 households	Projected annual number of households[b]
Household fires	5.8	464,000
Floods	3.4	272,000
Hurricanes and severe tropical storms	3.4	272,000
Tornadoes and severe windstorms	10.0	799,500
Earthquakes and severe tremors	1.8	138,000
Any of the four natural hazards	18.7	1,495,000
Any of the five hazards (including fires)	24.5	1,959,000

[a]A victimization is defined as any reported "experience" with a hazard event that involved injury to household members and/or damage to real or personal property of the household or its members.
[b]Based on estimated 79.5 million households as of 1980.
[c]Data from random-digit-dialing telephone survey. $N = 13,006$.

floods and hurricanes (and tropical storms), each victimizing more than a quarter of a million households annually, on the average. Earthquakes and tremors victimize least (at least in the 1970–1980 period) with a total coverage of about 138,000 households per annum. Note that victimization by any of the four hazards is about three times as frequent as household fire victimization: Fires are less than twice as frequent as either floods or hurricanes, three times more frequent than earthquakes, and about half as frequent as tornadoes and severe windstorms.

Compared with other types of noxious events that could affect households, the four natural hazard events studied taken together appeared to be less frequent than auto accidents, marital dissolutions, and unemployment, but more frequent than drug addictions, cases of alcoholism, or personal bankruptcies. In short, natural hazard events and the accompanying experiences are among the common "bad-luck" happenings that occur to the American population.

Although the spatial distribution of natural hazard events is fairly well known, their differential impact among social groups is not. The data from the screening interview provided information on how hazard events are distributed among various income levels, age groups, ethnic groups, and the like. No strong patterns appeared, however. Young households appear to be more likely victims of fires, floods, and tornadoes. Higher income households appeared to experience tornadoes and windstorms slightly more often than their poorer counterparts, but no other trends of note appeared, and even these noted trends are weak. In short, the five hazards appeared to be quite egalitarian, striking with about equal frequency among the several social classes and ethnic groups, and among renters as well as owners. Of course, regions specialized in types of natural hazard events, the association between East Coast and the Gulf States and hurricanes illustrating that well-known pattern. In short, vulnerability to hazard events appears to be more a matter of regional location than of position within the social structure of any region.

TABLE 1.2
Hazard-Generated Injuries and Damages (from Mail Survey)

	Hazard event				
	Fires	Floods	Hurricanes	Tornadoes	Earthquakes
Percentage with any injuries	9	8	2	2	2
Percentage with any damages	86	76	55	65	14
N =	(267)	(151)	(261)	(581)	(363)
Average dollar loss for those with any loss	$10,500	$10,500	$3,500	$2,500	$2,000
Median dollar loss for any loss	$2,500	$3,000	$800	$700	$1,000
Percentage of damage that is structural	39	31	40	46	55
N =	(218)	(112)	(142)	(365)	(44)

HAZARD-GENERATED INJURIES AND DAMAGES

Those households that claimed in telephone interviews that they had experienced hazard events were sent mail questionnaires that called for finer details on the injuries and damages sustained. The mail survey data on injuries and damages are discussed in detail in Chapter 5. Table 1.2 summarizes the major findings of the chapter: Injuries to household members occurred in 9% of household fires, 8% of floods, but in only about 2% of the other hazard events. All told, injuries were not very frequent. Deaths were even more unusual events connected with the natural hazard events of the 1970–1980 period, occurring in less than 1% of all the incidents.[1]

[1]Because households that were dissolved by deaths did not survive to be interviewed, these are undoubtedly underestimates of the true incidence of death caused by hazard events.

Damages to real and personal property holdings of the households were considerably more frequent. Nine out of ten household fires resulted in property damages that amounted on the average to $10,500. Three out of four flood events also resulted in damages that also averaged $10,500. About half of the hurricane experiences were accompanied by damages averaging $3,500, and two out of three of the tornado events involved average damages of $2,500. The earthquake and tremor experiences of the period 1970–1980 were, on the whole, trivial events, only 14% involving damages, averaging $2,000. Although the average amounts of damages inflicted appear to be high, these averages are very much influenced by a few households that experienced very large amounts of damages: The median values of damages are in every case much lower than the mean values.

Most of the damages inflicted were to the housing structures and dwelling units. Structural damage amounts ranged between 31% (for floods) and 55% (for earthquakes) of all damages claimed. The remaining damages were mainly to furnishings and personal property items.

When we consider the "total dollar cost" of household hazard experiences (defined as the costs incurred through injuries, deaths, or property damages), we find that there are few household characteristics that dispose a household to incur greater or smaller "total dollar costs." Fires and floods are likely to be more costly to owners (as opposed to renters): Structural damages to the dwellings of renters are borne by the structure owners. Higher income households experienced less damage from floods than lower income households, a finding for which no easy interpretation comes to mind. But the main factor appears to be the extent of the natural hazard event. Those events that involve other households in the neighborhood and community are likely to inflict higher total costs than those that involve only one or a few households. In other words, large-scale hazard events that are inflicted on many households appear to be likely to inflict larger total costs on any household.

SOURCES OF HELP

Americans have traditionally acted with great generosity toward the victims of natural hazards. A network of voluntary organizations has provided relief on the local level; a number of national organizations, notably the American National Red Cross, provide aid of a variety of sorts. In the past few decades, the federal government has also set up programs that are more-or-less automatically triggered into action when large-scale hazard events occur. On top of all that, individual households help one another in a variety of ways. Finally, insurance coverage is routinely purchased by households to cover some of the more common insurable risks. All of these sources of aid cannot fully restore the *status quo ante,* but individually and in combination, they can ease the road to recovery.

As shown in Chapter 6, the households that have suffered serious hazard events make considerable use of the sources of aid available to them. A summary of the coverage of various sources is given in Table 1.3. A majority of households suffering damages from fires, tornadoes, and hurricanes receive some reimbursement from insurance companies. Home-owner insurance policies routinely cover damages inflicted by high winds, wind-driven water, and household fires, and as shown in Table 1.3, a majority of households victimized by those hazard events receive some financial help from the coverages purchased. By and large, households were highly satisfied with their treatment at the hands of insurance companies, even though some complaints were registered that the payments were not high enough to cover replacement costs.

In contrast, few households received insurance payment help in the case of floods or earthquakes. In part, insurance coverage for those sources of damage was not available at "reasonable" prices during most of the period 1970–1980, and such coverage is not ordinarily a part of home-owner policies. In part, households are not inclined to take advantage of such coverage even when it is

TABLE 1.3

Sources and Types of Help Received by Households with Serious[a] Hazard Experiences

Source	Fires	Tornadoes	Hurricanes	Floods	Earthquakes
Percentage receiving some insurance payment	76	61	56	22	8
N =	(213)	(324)	(125)	(108)	(37)
Percentage receiving loans	6	5	7	13	9
N =	(218)	(365)	(144)	(112)	(44)
Number of informal sources of help	1.34	1.02	1.26	1.57	.39
N =	(222)	(342)	(142)	(119)	(50)
Number of contacts with agencies	.92	.56	.87	1.81	.42
N =	(213)	(333)	(136)	(109)	(52)
Receiving some help from one or more of above sources	94%	77%	79%	89%	36%
N =	(184)	(302)	(126)	(102)	(50)

[a]"Serious" events include those in which a household claimed nonzero damages.

available at "reasonable" prices. The result is that only small minorities (22% and 8%, respectively) receive any help from insurance payments for flood and earthquake damages.

Although only small minorities receive loans (ranging from 5% to 13%), this source of aid tends to be relied on by households that have suffered greater losses and those that are relatively poor. Note that loans are more likely to be used by flood and earthquake victims and that frequent sources are the low-cost federal loan programs (SBA in particular).

Grants and gifts (when given) tend to be smaller than loans but are received by more households. Especially important are the grants and gifts given to flood and earthquake victims. The activities of such national organizations as the Red Cross are especially visible in this connection.

The native generosity of Americans is shown most clearly in

the fact that informal help—usually in the form of labor and gifts—is frequently received by hazard victims. Formal agency contacts are also quite frequent. Especially impressive is the extent to which the households in every hazard experience cited the American Red Cross as a point of contact, especially flood victims.

Indeed, when we consider the combined coverages of insurance and other sources of help, strong majorities of all victims— with the exception of the victims of earthquakes—have received help from one or more sources, ranging from 94% in the case of household fires to a low of 77% for tornado victims. Especially impressive is the fact that there appears to be very little inequity in the distribution of aid. Among the natural hazard types, earthquakes appear to be poorly covered by any aid, possibly reflecting the types of earthquake experiences during the period under study.[2] The social distribution of aid appears to be quite even, with older households and more affluent households appearing slightly less likely to receive aid than their younger and poorer counterparts.

When the patterning of aid by source is examined in detail, it appears that the various sources are complementary. That is, when insurance payments play a major role, for example, loans and gifts from government agencies or private organizations do not and vice versa. In each case, the high coverage of aid of some kind is achieved by varying mixtures of aid from a variety of sources.

RECOVERY AND LINGERING EFFECTS

The final topic considered (Chapter 6) is the effects of the hazard experience that linger beyond the event itself. Most house-

---

[2]Most earth tremors during 1970–1980 were minor ones, inflicting only small amounts of damage. The San Fernando quake of 1971 was the only serious earthquake disaster occurring in this period.

holds are restored to full functioning within the space of a few days: At least, their dwellings are patched up enough for them to return to some semblance of workaday routine. Some are affected strongly enough by the event to experience depression, and others borrow money to the extent that their debt burden is seriously increased.

Our analyses indicate that feelings of depression and of burdens of debt increase both with the amount of debt involved and also with contacts with all sorts of agencies. Although it is to be expected that a family that doubles its mortgage will feel somewhat put out about the increased payments and perhaps the resulting longer pay period, it is not clear why contact with agencies should result in such feelings. Perhaps these findings simply reflect the fact that those with more troubles seek more help.

Conclusion

Experiences with natural hazard events are relatively rare but sufficiently frequent to affect about 1% of American households annually. A network of institutionally defined aid, as well as insurance companies and informal helping out, is available to victimized households. A majority take advantage of the help offered by the aid system, but for some, aid is only a buffer between themselves and the burdens of the experience that have to be borne nevertheless.

CHAPTER 2

Estimating Hazard Events and Consequences through a Victimization Survey

INTRODUCTION

Every year many lives are lost and much property is damaged by the ravages of natural hazards. There is some evidence, moreover, that the magnitude of these losses, especially to property, has increased substantially in constant dollars in recent years, mainly because economic growth has tended to concentrate more and more persons and property in high-risk areas (Cochrane, 1975; Dacy and Kunreuther, 1969; White and Haas, 1975). In addition, the past decade has produced several very-large-scale disaster events that imposed severe burdens on the public treasury for relief and rehabilitation, for example, Hurricane Agnes in 1973.[1] Spurred by these rising costs and by other reasons, federal hazards policy has been shifting away from providing relief and fostering rehabilitation in the aftermath of disasters, and toward developing strategies that are aimed at mitigating hazard risks before disasters strike. Perhaps, in the long run, a vigorous and scientifically informed program of risk mitigation will reduce substantially, as

[1]Although Agnes occurred in calendar year 1972, federal expenditures were incurred in fiscal year 1973.

11

hoped, the need for relief and rehabilitation programs. In the foreseeable future, however, it is likely that policies involving direct relief for and rehabilitation of victims will figure prominently in the repertoire of federal disaster responses.

Precise estimates of the total costs of disaster relief and rehabilitation to the nation are difficult to construct,[2] in part because of the many agencies, public and private, that shoulder some share of the burdens. Also, total costs are difficult to estimate because losses are both direct and indirect; indeed, many of the indirect losses (e.g., revenues lost because of hazard-related unemployment) go unrecorded in most of the easily accessible records. Nevertheless, it is possible to arrive at some estimates of at least major parts of the costs inflicted by natural hazards:

1. For 1970–1979 (estimated), the annual federal expenditure for "disaster relief and insurance" averaged about $610 million per year (Office of Management and Budget, 1978:70). Outlays have varied from a low of $300 million in 1970 to a high of $1.6 billion in 1973, the fiscal year of Agnes. The figures cited here include only direct costs to the federal government and do not include any of the indirect costs, which range in source from income tax deductions for uninsured casualty losses[3] to productivity declines resulting from the interruptions of normal economic activity that often follow major disasters (Cochrane, 1975).

2. In the most recent years, actual federal disaster expenditures have greatly exceeded the estimated expenditures, owing to several very widespread or highly destructive disasters. Federal relief expenditures for the Johnstown flash flood of July 1977 were about $215 million (National Oceanic and Atmospheric Administration, 1977:4). The western drought of 1976–1977 was also very expensive to the federal government. Through July 1977,

---

[2] See Federal Emergency Management Administration, *Special Statistical Summary* (1982), Washington, D.C., for a detailed analysis of deficiencies in existing data bases.

[3] Dacy and Kunreuther (1969:224) estimated that federal tax revenues lost through the deduction allowance amounted to $255 million in 1965, the last year for which data are available.

federal drought assistance to California alone totaled $37 million in loans and $17 million in outright grants (Comptroller General of the United States, 1977:38–39). These figures, although high in an absolute sense, are dwarfed by the total cost of that drought to the nation. The Comptroller General's report estimates that drought-related losses in California agriculture were about $2.4 billion in 1977 alone.

3. Disaster costs to the federal government represent only a fractional share of the total government disaster expenditure; some additional share is borne directly by state and local governments. At present, the largest bulk of federal disaster assistance is dispensed under the provisions of the Disaster Relief Act of 1974 (PL 93-288). That act states specifically that the federal effort is to "supplement the efforts and available resources of states, local governments, and disaster relief organizations." Unfortunately, there appears to be no reliable information available on the disaster-related expenditures of state and local governments, so the size of their share cannot be estimated.

4. In general, governmental expenditures for disaster relief cover only some portions of the loss—those that are not covered by private insurance. According to data supplied by the American Insurance Association, disaster-related payments by its member companies exceeded $417 million in 1977 and have averaged more than $350 million annually during the years of 1967–1977 (Walter Swift, private communication).

5. Some disaster relief is provided, not by government or by private insurance, but by private or semiprivate relief organizations, of which the American National Red Cross (ANRC) is by far the largest and most active. ANRC expenditures for disaster relief averaged about $9.3 million annually for the years 1959–1964, increased to an annual average of about $18.1 million for the years 1965–1970, and have averaged roughly $27.9 million per year from 1970 to 1977 (*ANRC Annual Summary of Disaster Services Activities*, 1959–1977).

The figures cited in the previous paragraphs represent some (probably rather small) fraction of the *known direct* costs to the nation of natural hazards. Other costs are *indirect*, for example, opportunity costs paid because the dollars spend on disaster relief are not spent on something else, the costs imposed in developing and maintaining hazard warning systems, the costs for research, the costs of constructing and maintaining disaster control installations (such as dams, seawalls, and dikes), and the costs that result from the stricter building standards enacted for risk mitigation, etc.

Some (possibly large) share of the total costs is simply *unknown* because the people who shoulder these costs—the hazard victims themselves (or their friends and families)—may never apply for federal assistance, may never come to the attention of the Red Cross, or may never file an insurance claim for compensation. These victims would not appear in any agency's records, so their losses are not accounted for in the data mentioned here.

Given the various difficult-to-estimate quantities that go into cost estimation for natural hazards, it is apparent that no one can state with any certainty just what the total annual costs to the nation are. Cochrane (1975:1) cited a figure "in excess of $5 billion per year"; and the White and Haas (1975) estimate is $10 billion per year; certainly, these estimates seem at least reasonable, given what has been said in the previous pages. Thus, one would apparently be safe in characterizing natural hazards in the United States as at least a multibillion-dollar yearly problem.

RESEARCH STRATEGY

Constructing accurate estimates of the total costs of hazard events in the United States would necessarily be a complicated undertaking that would employ the skills of accounting, economics, and survey research, among other fields. In any event, the task is beyond the goals of this research. Our more modest aim is to construct estimates of one of the major components of the total costs of disaster events, those borne by private households directly through injuries and household property damages. Of course, part of the household cost is known through payments made by insurance companies, grants and gifts made by public and private agencies, and loans from various sources. The share of total losses reimbursed through such mechanisms is, however, unknown. Certainly, some costs (possibly a large proportion) are borne directly by households and are those for which no compensating payments are made. These "hidden" costs are an integral part of the estimates undertaken in this volume.

The overriding purpose of the research reported here is to estimate the burden that hazard events inflict on households and to determine how the costs of natural hazards are distributed among such victims. Although there are now several sophisticated studies bearing on the long-term effects of disasters or hazards on whole communities, very little research has focused on the effects of disasters or hazards on the individual victims, least of all over the long run (that is, beyond the immediate postemergency phase). Given the general magnitude of the natural hazards problem in the United States, it is somewhat surprising that better data on hazard victimization are not available for policy planning or hazard management.

Some of the questions to which we will provide answers are: What are the rates of victimization from natural hazards of various sorts? How many households suffer hazard losses in a given time span? What are the sizes of the average losses? Of those who are victimized, what proportion receive relief assistance? How do average losses from natural hazards compare with other types of casualty loss, for example, from home fires? Are there unintentional inequities in present relief and rehabilitation efforts, so that some victims are more likely to receive aid than others? And for those who receive assistance, how are the funds spent? What is the average "recovery time" for individual, family, and business victims? How long does it take for victims to be restored to their predisaster condition? Finally, what are the overall costs of natural hazards to their victims? And, of these costs, what share is covered by governmental assistance, what share by private insurance, what share by voluntary relief agencies, and what share by the resources of the victims themselves?

Many of these questions appear to be so elementary to our understanding of the relevant policy issues concerning environmental risk management that it is surprising that so few answers have been furnished by previous research. The main reason for this apparent information gap is that social scientists have been usually (if not exclusively) attracted to the study of the effects of the largest and most cataclysmic hazard events. Major tornado outbreaks, the largest floods (dramatic flash floods, especially), and the major hurricanes have attracted most of the attention of researchers. True, these catastrophic events are the ones that also attract the most attention from the media and from policymakers. Indeed, a very good case can be made that our disaster policies have been largely reactive to such events, major changes in federal legislation usually following after some catastrophic event.

However important such catastrophic events appear to be, they are only a small, highly unrepresentative, and select subset of the total set of destructive hazards. Indeed, it is useful to distinguish between *natural disasters* (catastrophic natural hazard occurrences that involve widespread damage and injuries) and *natural hazard events* (any untoward hydrological, meteorological, or geological occurrence that causes sudden and unanticipated loss to at least one person). If we use this distinction, it is clear that prior social science literature has dealt almost exclusively with natural disasters, whereas this monograph focuses on victimization by natural hazard events, regardless of whether the event in question qualifies as a "disaster." In other words, a family suffering, say, a $5,000 flood loss qualifies, in our minds, as a hazard victim worthy of study: Whether that family was the only family suffering loss in the flood, or only one of hundreds of families suffering similar losses is, from the point of view of that family (and of this monograph), more-or-less immaterial.

To give some concreteness to the relative scales involved,

between 1960 and 1970 about 8,500 tornadoes occurred in the United States. Of this total number, somewhat more than half (about 4,300) did damage in excess of $5,000, a nontrivial loss if suffered by a single family or an individual victim. And yet, of the 4,000 or so tornadoes causing damages of this magnitude or higher, only 129 were serious enough to receive a Small Business Administration disaster declaration, a mere 25 received a presidential disaster declaration, and no more than perhaps 5 or 10 received any serious or sustained research attention. Now, obviously, the scores of tornadoes receiving declarations and research attention were, far and away, the most serious tornado disasters of the period. But it is equally obvious that the net suffering and loss produced by the thousands of nondeclared and unstudied tornadoes might easily equal or exceed the losses due to the several dozen genuine tornado "disasters." Any study of victimization by natural hazard, then, must obviously be concerned with the thousands of routine, "garden variety" hazard events as well as with natural disasters. The focus in prior literature on disasters has meant that social science has actually had very little to say about the questions posed above.

The policy issues posed by the above distinction are by no means trivial. At present, the official "disaster declaration" is the trigger for most (although not all) of the federal disaster-relief effort. In theory, a declaration is issued when the magnitude of destruction exceeds the state's or local community's ability to respond. In fact, large-scale and well-publicized disasters almost invariably receive a declaration, whereas small-scale and relatively anonymous ones do not. It is certainly possible that the aggregate loss due to the many thousands of these small-scale events exceeds (possibly even by orders of magnitude) the aggregate loss due to the few officially declared catastrophes, and if that proves to be the case, then we would be dealing with a federal policy mechanism that is designed and implemented so as to respond to the smaller part of the overall environmental hazard problem.

RESEARCH DESIGN

The research findings contained in this monograph were derived from a large-scale data-collection effort that was designed to provide estimates of the injuries and damages sustained from natural hazard events by households in the context of their living quarters. By *households*, we mean groups of persons who live together in the same dwelling unit and who, in one way or another, share their living expenses. Although the typical household of today is a married couple and dependent children, there are also many single-person households, some households consisting of persons unrelated by marriage or blood, and some households that are mixtures of kin and nonkin.

Under this definition of our target population as households, we exclude all persons who are not members of households: the 2% of the adult population who live in group quarters, are hospitalized, or are in prison or in the military. These exclusions involve a minor portion of the population and are routinely adopted in sample surveys in order to simplify data collection.

The injuries and damages experienced by households to be estimated are those suffered by members of the household in the context of their dwelling units, excluding injuries and damages that might occur in work places, schools, while traveling in public places, and so on. Again, the purpose of the exclusion is to simplify data collection. Thus, the focus here is very much on household losses due to natural hazard events.

The general research problems addressed here (and consequently the general research design) are similar to those addressed by students of criminal victimization. In an earlier era, the study of crime was more-or-less confined to crimes reported to or detected by the police. From the beginning, there was a recognition that such crime constituted only a fractional share of the total crime, but whether the fraction was large or small was largely unknown. Also, it might be supposed that some victims of crime would be more likely than others to report their victimization to the police. Thus, crimes known to the police were not only a fractional subset of all crime, but possibly a biased one as well. In the mid-1960s, the method of measuring crime victimization by surveys was developed, whereby rates of crime were estimated by asking probability samples of the population whether they had been victimized over the previous year. These studies showed that survey-reported crimes exceeded officially reported crimes by factors ranging from 1.5 to 10, depending on the crime type. Much victimization by crime was "hidden" from official view.

The case of victimization by natural hazards is similar in important respects. Traditionally, the victims studied are those who have come to the attention of one or another relief agency or who otherwise appear in some official record. Whether this is a large or a small fraction of the total victimized population has been largely unknown. Whether some victims are more likely than others to come forth for aid or be granted help, or in other words, whether there are intentional or unintentional inequities in the relief effort, has also been unknown. Adapting the method of the victimization survey to the case of victimization by natural hazards is therefore straightforward: Using a probability sample of the entire population of households, one can compute a victimization rate, and as in the case of the crime surveys, the victims identified in this process can be queried about the details and circumstances of their losses. Such, in brief, is the design of the research whose findings are reported in this volume.

The validity of this design, of course, rests heavily on the ability of household members to retrieve from their memories information on whether the household has experienced a natural hazard event and, if so, the details of the associated injuries and damages. It stands to reason that major disasters involving large areas and many households will be remembered as salient life experiences. Any reader who has such experiences will undoubtedly concur. The major problem lies in whether lesser natural hazard events will be recalled at all and whether the details of losses can be recalled with sufficient accuracy to serve as the bases for estimates.

Although natural hazard events may cause billions of dollars annually in losses, only very small proportions of the total U.S. household population are victimized in any given period of time. Victimization is a rare event, and only very small minorities experience any one or any combination of hazard events in any decade. Hence, in any random sample of the population, households that could give us information on hazards losses are necessarily only some small proportion of all the households contacted. This distribution of hazard experiences led to a two-stage sampling design. The first stage consisted of a large probability sample of telephone-owning households, which we interviewed primarily to locate a subsample of persons who had experienced natural disasters during the previous 11 years. The second stage consisted of follow-up mail surveys of all households who had experienced one or more hazard events. The mail survey queried victimized households about the details of injuries and damages suffered, as well as information on the aftermath effects of the experiences.

The first-stage telephone survey contacted more than 13,000 households with a short interview that for most households lasted about 10 minutes. Most households (more than 85%) in the United States have a home phone. Of course, those who did not have a phone in November and December 1980 fell outside the first-stage sampling operation, a sampling bias that resulted in an underrepresentation of poor households, older households, and single-person households. The telephone numbers used were generated by a computer routine that ensures that unlisted and newly listed phone numbers will be included. Sampling and interviewing on the phone were conducted under subcontract to Audits and Surveys, Inc., using the interview schedule that is reproduced in Appendix B.

The period 1970–1980 was chosen as the base period for our study largely because our preliminary estimates of the incidence of victimization (as discussed in detail in Appendix A) led us to believe that a base period would have to be at least that long to produce a sufficiently large sample of victims. The study is therefore further biased to the extent that the 1970s were an uncharacteristic decade.

Any adult member of the household qualified as someone who could provide information on the natural hazard experiences of the household. When our household informant indicated that the household had experienced a natural hazard event during the base period, some basic information about the experience was collected, along with the mailing address of the household.

Interviews with the 13,000 households in the first stage of interviewing uncovered more than 2,600 households that had experienced one or more natural hazard events during the base period. As described in the next chapter, most of these households were mailed one or more questionnaires that asked for more detailed information about the experiences. The mail survey was also conducted under subcontract to Audits and Surveys, Inc. The questionnaire used is reprinted in Appendix B.

The mailed questionnaire covered a number of topics: Injuries and deaths experienced, property losses, sources of financial aid and other forms of help, time of recovery, some information on aftermath effects, and the socioeconomic characteristics of the household.

THE HAZARDS STUDIED

Only a limited number of types of natural hazards could be studied. Some were so rare (e.g., soil expansion) or so geographically specific (e.g., tsunamis) that only one or two experiences could be expected even in a sample as large as 13,000. Others (e.g., heavy snowfalls) were very frequent but only rarely produced major losses. Our strategy was to pick those hazards that were comparatively frequent and often quite serious: hurricanes, tornadoes, floods, and earthquakes. In order to provide a comparative frame, we also included household fires as events that are fairly frequent, often serious, and clearly localized within dwellings. These are also the natural hazards that receive the most attention in the disaster strategy of public officials.

PLAN OF THE MONOGRAPH

The present chapter has provided a brief overview of the design of and the rationale for this research. In the following chapter, the design and execution of the study are described in more detail. As the more detailed discussion makes plain, there are three major areas of inquiry that can be pursued with our data. First, the results from the screening interview can be used to estimate the rates at which U.S. households are victimized by natural hazards events. With the same data, it is also possible to explore the correlates of hazard victimization, that is, to ascertain which types of households are more-and-less prone to suffering a hazard-related loss. These analyses are described in Chapter 4.

As noted above, the victimized households located in the first phase were sent a follow-up questionnaire through the mail. The results obtained from the mail survey bear, first, on the nature and extent of household hazard losses and, second, on the nature of the ensuing recovery. Chapter 5 reports our analysis of hazard loss, focusing mainly on personal injury and property damages. In Chapter 6, our attention turns to the process of recovery; here, the focus is on the flow of relief and assistance to hazard victims.

CHAPTER 3

The Victimization Survey

Data Collection and Survey Implementation

Data on victimization by household fires and natural hazards were gathered in two stages, following the general logic of the design discussed in the previous chapter. Previous disaster literature had centered on very selective and possibly unique victim populations (i.e., on the victims of well-publicized disasters). In contrast, we hoped to generate a survey closely approximating a probability sample of the *total* hazard-victimized population of the United States. Such a population is, of course, unlisted, and no known sampling frame of the requisite scope exists. For these reasons, the first stage of data collection was a very large telephone screening interview, which was used (1) to estimate hazard victimization rates for hazards of various types, and (2) to locate a probability sample of victims for purposes of a more extensive and detailed follow-up questionnaire.

The screening interview was based on a random sample of all telephone owning households in the United States, obtained using random-digit-dialing (RDD) sampling methods (Groves and Kahn, 1978). RDD sampling methods generate random samples of telephone numbers that can then be used as the basis for a telephone survey. The RDD methods include all working telephone numbers, including unlisted and newly installed telephones. The phone interviews were relatively short (average duration of about

23

10 minutes). Respondents were asked whether their households had experienced any household fires, floods, hurricanes, tornadoes, or earthquakes during the previous 11 years. A "yes" to any of the questions in this sequence was followed up by brief questions about the deaths, injuries, and dollar losses incurred in these incidents. All respondents were also asked a few standard sociodemographic questions. The respondents were then asked to participate in a more extensive follow-up study.

The hazard victims identified in the telephone interviews who agreed to participate in the follow-up study were subsequently mailed a questionnaire that requested more detailed information on the losses incurred, insurance coverage (if any), sources of relief and rehabilitation aid, and other matters concerning their victimization. These mailed questionnaires constituted the second phase of the data collection.

The present chapter describes more fully the survey methods and field procedures employed in these two phases of the research. The response rates are also calculated and analyzed. Finally, some basic descriptive information about the samples is presented.

THE SCREENER TELEPHONE INTERVIEW

The first stage of the study, the screener interview, was designed both to provide estimates of household hazard-victimization rates and to locate a sample of disaster victims for later in-depth follow-up. At this stage, our concern was to sample enough households to provide reliable estimates of the victimization rates and to produce a large enough number of victims for the second stage. An analysis of existing data sources (see Appendix A) provided an initial "best estimate" that about 15% of all U.S. households would have experienced natural disasters (including household fires) during an 11-year period, although the uncertainties in this estimate were rather large. Budgetary constraints also dictated a follow-up mail sample of not more than about 2,000–2,500 cases. These considerations thus suggested a sample size of about 13,000–14,000 cases for the screening interview: A sample of this scale would certainly provide reliable estimates of hazard victimization rates (whatever they happened to be) and would also yield sufficient cases for follow-up even if the true rate of victimization proved to be well below the "best guess" of about 15%.

The sample for telephone interviewing was obtained through a randomly generated list of telephone numbers assembled by Survey Sampling, Inc., working under contract with Audits and Surveys, Inc. The RDD procedure that was followed yields a simple random sample of all U.S. households that have telephones in their dwellings. Some households do not have a telephone, and the RDD sample is correspondingly biased. The numbers of households missed are very small. The efficiency, reliability, and cost-effectiveness of RDD sampling for a screening process of this sort is well documented in the survey literature (e.g., Dillman, 1978; Groves and Kahn, 1978).

Approximately 36,000 actual phone numbers—or about three times the number needed—were included in the initial screener sample because it was known that many of these phone numbers would be ineligible (i.e., nonworking numbers, business telephones, and the like). The final disposition of these 36,000 is shown in Table 3.1. As expected, slightly less than half (43.3%) of the numbers proved ineligible or for other reasons had to be excluded. Over half of these were nonworking numbers (43.6%) or business numbers (11.0%). An additional 45% remained uncontacted (no answer or busy signal) after repeated callback attempts. (Three attempts were made on each number before giving up.)

In telephone interviewing, unanswered numbers are inherently ambiguous. In some cases, a nonworking number will, when dialed, result in a recorded message stating that the number is nonworking or unassigned. These appear in Table 3.1 as "not a working number." In other cases, however, an unassigned number will appear to ring but go unanswered and is thus indistinguishable from a not-at-home respondent. Thus, "no answer" includes both some nonworking numbers and "not at homes." For this

TABLE 3.1
Disposition of Screener Telephone Interview Attempts (N = 36,108 Random-Digit Phone Numbers)

Phone numbers never contacted	15,622		43.3%
Not a working number		43.6%	
Business phone		11.0%	
No answer		39.3%	
Busy signal		6.0%	
Phone numbers with at least one contact	20,486		56.7%
Adult respondent not available		7.8%	
Language problem		2.7%	
Respondent refusal		26.1%	
Completed interview		63.5%	
		100%	= (36,018)

reason, the actual "response rate" in a telephone survey is impossible to calculate; the appropriate denominator for such a rate is inherently ambiguous. The more commonly reported figure is thus the cooperation rate among contacts made with eligible households or respondents.

In the end, the phone interviewers made contact with 20,486 (57.6%) of the initial 36,108 numbers. This is somewhat higher than the average "contact rate" reported in the survey literature. Of the 20,486 interviewer contacts, 13,005 resulted in completed screening interviews, a completion rate of 63.5%. The largest source of noncompletion was outright refusal to be interviewed, amounting to 26.1% of the contacted cases. Refusal rates reported in the literature vary from about 10% to about 35%; our rate was thus on the high side of average for phone interviewing of this sort. In about 8% of the cases, there was no adult respondent available when contact was made, and in the remaining 3% of the cases, noncompletion resulted from language difficulties.

The screener interview instrument is reproduced in Appendix B. It was a fairly short interview in which respondents were first asked if they had experienced a household fire, flood, hurricane, tornado, or earthquake during the 1970–1980 period. If the respondent answered "yes," the interview continued with a few questions about the year (or years) of the event(s), any deaths or injuries, and rough damage estimates. For most, the interview ended with a small number of questions about the demographic characteristics of the household. A 10% random subsample (N = 1,245) was also asked an additional series of questions concerning experiences with other types of calamities.

All told, 3,292 respondents indicated some experience with one or more of the five hazards over the previous 11 years—a "take rate" of just over 25%, or much higher than the originally anticipated 15%. Each of these 3,292 was requested to participate in a follow-up survey. About 2,500 agreed at this point. They were then asked to provide names and mailing addresses. During the ensuing weeks, these families were mailed follow-up question-naires, a separate questionnaire being sent for each disaster expe-rience reported.

Fieldwork for the screener interviewing was done by Audits and Surveys, Inc., under subcontract to the University of Mas-sachusetts. Its interviewing staff completed the 13,000 telephone interviews during a three-week period in November and Decem-ber 1980. The phone interviewing was done by means of a CATI (computer-assisted telephone-interviewing) system. CATI inter-viewing uses a computer to drive the interviewing sequence. The computer program dials a phone number that is part of the sample to be used, records whether or not the telephone is answered, and then flashes each question on a cathode ray screen for the inter-viewer to read into the phone. Answers to each question are re-corded by the interviewer, who types in the appropriate response code into a computer terminal. The CATI program checks the response for consistency and appropriateness and then flashes the next question. The responses are stored on tape or disk and are immediately available for tabulation and analysis. The CATI sys-tem also recycles any unanswered telephone numbers and redials them at other times. The use of such a data-gathering system not only facilitates the interviewing process but also allows quick access to the final screener data base.

Initial analysis of the screener data revealed that 3,292 households (25.3%) reported an experience with one or more of the five disaster types during the 1970–1980 period. Specifically, there were 553 households reporting household fires, 328 reporting floods, 663 reporting hurricanes, 1,440 reporting tornadoes, and 977 reporting earthquakes.

As we show in later chapters, the numbers given above for tornadoes and earthquakes are somewhat misleading. The question for tornadoes asked about "tornado or severe windstorm," and that for earthquake about "earthquakes or tremors." Thus, the "nets" being cast were rather wider in these two cases than in the other three. Preliminary analysis also revealed, as might be expected, that large proportions of tornado and earthquake experiences were accompanied by no damage, injuries, or deaths. (See Chapter 4 for a detailed analysis of the death, injury, and damage rates by type of hazard.)

As indicated, about 2,500 of the 3,292 hazard victims located in the screener agreed to participate in the follow-up; the rest declined. Further analysis revealed that most of the "refusals" were among persons with essentially trivial hazard experiences—experiences generating no deaths or injuries and minor or nonexistent amounts of dollar loss. Among the roughly 800 refusals, however, were some 203 households whose hazard experience was apparently not trivial, and we were anxious to include as many of them as possible in the follow-up study. Accordingly, the data collection subcontractor was instructed to recontact by telephone the respondents from these households and attempt to persuade them to participate in the study. These conversion efforts produced an additional 78 households for the mail survey, bringing the total sample size for the mail follow-up to 2,603 households.

THE MAIL SURVEY

The fieldwork for the second phase of the study was also handled by Audits and Surveys, Inc., as subcontractor, and it began with a questionnaire mailing to 2,603 households. Each household received one questionnaire for each hazard event that had been reported in the phone interview. The first page of each questionnaire listed the type of event (flood, fire, etc.) and the year of the event as reported in the screener interview. The respondents were asked first to confirm this information and then to complete the questionnaire with regard to that one event. To emphasize, the households reporting multiple hazard events were sent multiple questionnaires. Over all sampled households, the number of questionnaires sent varied from 1 to 39, with most households receiving only a single questionnaire.[1]

The initial mailing was followed a few weeks later by a postcard reminder to nonresponding households urging their cooperation. The response rate after this first follow-up mailing was fairly low, standing at about 30%. The early returns suggested that many nonresponding households had had relatively minor hazard experiences. Because the disaster histories of these households was of lesser concern to the purpose of the research, it was decided, rather than continuing to pester these "less interesting" respondents through additional follow-up mailings, to adopt a more focused follow-up strategy for the third mailing. The relevant details of the strategy we adopted are as follows.

Any nonresponding household that had indicated either a flood or a fire experience in the screener was sent a second set of questionnaires, one for each fire or flood event. This strategy was followed irrespective of the reported damages and loss, for three related reasons. First, we had fewer fire and flood victims from the screening interviews than we had hoped for. Second, the number of "trivials" among fire and flood victims was known from the screener to be relatively low. Finally, relatively few households had reported multiple fire or flood experiences. In the third mail-

---

[1]The maximum number of questionnaires sent varied over hazard types. The high figure, 39 questionnaires, was registered for tornadoes. One earthquake household received 33 questionnaires, and one flood household, 21 questionnaires. As indicated in the text, however, the vast majority of the households (over 90%) received only a single questionnaire.

TABLE 3.2

Disposition of Hazard Events Reported on the Screener
in the Mail Survey

	Total	Fire	Flood	Hurricane	Tornado	Earthquake
A. Household reports						
Total households reporting a hazard event	3,292	553	328	663	1,440	977
Total events reported	6,177	587	482	933	2,598	1,577
Average per household		1.06	1.47	1.41	1.80	1.61
Percentage of events in						
Noncooperating households	17.7	7.0	7.3	15.5	37.6	32.6
Excluded through sampling	15.0	0.5	0.6	12.0	20.6	17.3
Eligible for survey	67.3	92.5	92.1	72.5	41.8	50.1
Total events eligible for survey	4,158	507	399	652	1,652	948
Percentage undelivered	4.7	6.3	4.8	4.6	4.3	4.7
B. Event reports						
Total events eligible for inclusion in survey	(3,961)	(475)	(380)	(622)	(1,581)	(903)
Completed questionnaire (%)	33.1	44.0	34.5	34.2	29.5	32.3
Completed phone interview (%)	7.4	9.3	4.7	7.7	6.8	8.6
Never happened[a] (%)	13.6	7.8	11.3	12.9	15.9	14.3
Refused (%)	8.4	11.2	8.2	9.2	8.3	6.5
No response (%)	37.4	27.8	41.3	36.0	39.4	38.2
Overall response rate[b] (%)	54.1	61.1	50.5	54.8	52.2	55.2

[a] Respondent indicated event never occurred or was too trivial for response.
[b] (Total complete questionnaires + phone interview + "never happened")/total eligible events.

ing, then, all flood and fire households that had not responded to the first two mailings were sent additional questionnaires. Included in the packet was a second covering letter urging their cooperation in the study.

Hurricane, tornado, and earthquake victims were treated differently. Any household that reported a nontrivial experience with one of these three hazards (that is, that reported at least some injury or property loss in the screener), and that had not responded after the second mailing, was sent a second packet of questionnaires, as in the fire and flood case described above. These packets also contained a second covering letter. The remaining hurricane, tornado, and earthquake nonresponders—those reporting no damage or injury in the screener interview—were sampled, and only the sampled households received the third mailing. Sampling of the "trivial" events, we felt, was justified because they would generate little or no useful information on hazard victimization. Sampling in this fashion also reduced the number of questionnaires that some nonresponding households received, so that the task of completing the questionnaires became less burdensome. Details on the numbers of events sampled, by hazard type, are given in Table 3.2.

Several weeks after the third follow-up mailing, a number of households still had not responded. Each of these households was contacted by telephone and urged to complete and return the questionnaire. In cases where this telephone "reminder" proved inadequate and the household's questionnaire(s) still had not been received after a reasonable time, an effort was made to gather the relevant data directly over the phone. For this purpose, the mail questionnaire was edited down into two shorter versions. The first, which was used only for households whose experiences had been "trivial," omitted most of the questions on damage, injuries, insurance coverage, and reimbursements. The second, used with households reporting nontrivial experiences, was only slightly different from the mail questionnaire itself, the changes consisting mostly of amended instructions and response categories to provide a more appropriate format for a telephone interview. A total of 348 phone interviews were done, of which 234 concerned trivial events and 114 dealt with nontrivial events.

Fieldwork was completed during the summer of 1981. At that point, a total of 1,694 households had responded to the hazard survey, either by returning questionnaires or by completing the phone interview.

The final disposition of all households in this second phase of the study is shown in Table 3.3. A total of 3,292 households initially reported a hazard experience on the screener interview and were therefore eligible to be included in the follow-up survey. However, the final sample size for the mail survey was only 2,603 households because of the exclusion of those refusing to cooperate, as discussed above. Of the 2,603 households who agreed to cooperate, 108 (or 4.1%) never received their questionnaires because at each mailing their packets were returned as undeliverable. Attempts to confirm these addresses were unsuccessful by the close of the fieldwork.

Of the households eligible to provide a response, some 315 (or 12.6%) responded by indicating that the specified hazard had never occurred. The "never happened" category includes those who later realized that the year of the event was incorrect (earlier than 1970 and thus ineligible for our study), those who insisted that the hazard experience was so minor as not to qualify as a "disaster," and those who responded simply that the hazard had never happened. Despite all efforts, 32.1% of the initial households never responded at all. The remaining 1,379 households completed one or more hazard questionnaires or phone interviews, for a completion rate against the initial sample of 55.3%. If the 315 households falling in the "never happened" category are counted as responders rather than nonresponders, the final overall completion rate for the mail survey is 67.9%.

Table 3.3 also shows the response rates by type of hazard. In most cases, the variation in response by hazard type is modest and insignificant. As shown, 21% of the potential sample refused further cooperation with the study (by refusing to reveal their mailing addresses) at the time of the screening interview: This refusal

TABLE 3.3
Final Disposition of Sample Households

	Total[a]	Fire	Flood	Hurricane	Tornado	Earthquake
Total HH reporting a hazard event in the screener	(3,292)	(553)	(328)	(663)	(1,440)	(977)
Percentage noncooperating at the time of screening	20.9	13.6	16.8	19.0	19.7	25.3
Total HH mailed a questionnaire packet	(2,603)	(478)	(273)	(537)	(1,156)	(730)
Percentage never delivered	4.1	6.3	5.1	4.1	3.5	4.9
Total HH eligible to respond	(2,495)	(458)	(259)	(515)	(1,115)	(694)
Complete (%)	55.3	56.3	56.0	53.4	52.6	58.1
Never happened[b] (%)	12.6	7.6	8.5	12.4	15.5	12.0
No response (%)	32.1	36.0	35.5	34.2	31.8	30.0
Overall response rate[c] (%)	67.9	63.9	64.5	65.8	68.1	70.1

[a]Households could, and did, report more than one type of hazard occurrence, as well as multiple occurrences of a single type. Thus, the total households reporting an event (3,292) is much less than the sum of the number reporting each type of event (3,961).
[b]Respondent indicated that all reported events never occurred or were too trivial for response.
[c](Total households with complete questionnaire + "never happened")/eligible HHs.

rate varied from a low of 13.6% among fire victims to a high of 25.3% among earthquake victims. Of those agreeing to cooperate, 4% never received a questionnaire packet owing to bad addresses (packets returned as undeliverable): This figure varied narrowly from 3.5% to 6.3%. There was also modest variation by hazard type in the overall completion rate, ranging from a low of 52.6% to a high of 58.1%. The sharpest pattern revealed in this panel of the table is in the "never happened" category, with higher proportions registered for the more diffuse hazards (hurricane, tornado, and earthquake). Clearly, many people "experienced" such events without ever being "victimized" by them, a point confirmed in later analyses.

The lower third of Table 3.3 presents the final response rates of the households in the hazard survey. This rate is defined as the total number of households responding at some level (either by completing a questionnaire or a phone interview or by responding that the reported event should not be included in the study), divided by the total number of households eligible to respond. Again, there is little variation in this rate by type of hazard, hovering around two-thirds in all categories.

THE EVENT SAMPLE

To this point, the discussion has been based on the victimized households located in the screener interview. During fieldwork, the household was necessarily the basic unit for tracking the data collection effort. However, the final sample was a sample of hazard events as well as a sample of victimized households; indeed, the 3,292 victims located in the screener reported a total of 6,177 discrete hazard occurrences, for an average of nearly two events per victimized household. In the next several pages, we discuss the final disposition of the 6,177 reported hazard occurrences; the relevant data are shown in Section B of Table 3.2.

The first set of figures in the table shows the number of households reporting a hazard of each type, as well as the total number of hazard experiences reported. It should be noted that any single household could report multiple types of disasters as well as multiple occurrences of a single type. For this reason, the total number of households reporting any hazard event (N = 3,292) is much smaller than the sum of the number of households reporting each type of event, that is, the sum of the first column of Table 3.2 (N = 3,961).

The average number of occurrences varied substantially by type of disaster. Most fire victims reported one and only one fire experience; the average number of fires reported by households was 1.06. The averages for floods and hurricanes were similar (1.47 and 1.41, respectively) and were higher than that shown for fires. The highest averages appear for earthquake (1.61) and tornado (1.80), again, presumably because of the broad definition of hazards used in these two cases.

The second set of figures in Table 3.2 presents the percentages of total events that were either excluded or included in the follow-up sample. Overall, 67.3% of all reported events were covered by the mail survey. Events were excluded from the sample either because they were reported by households that refused to cooperate further in the study (17.7% of all events) or because the events were not selected in the sampling process described earlier (15.0% of all events). The percentages of events excluded by sampling was greatest among hurricane (12%), tornado (21%), and earthquake (17%) events, as would be expected from the sampling strategy.[2] There was also a large difference by type of hazard in the number of events excluded because of respondent refusal, with almost one out of every three tornado and earthquake events being lost for this reason. Because Table 3.3 showed only a small difference in the household noncooperation rate among tornado and earthquake victims, the large differences shown here can reflect only the higher average number of total events reported by tornado and earthquake households. It is clear, in any case, that

---

[2]A small number of fire and flood events were excluded because their questionnaires were never sent for some reason, not because of sampling.

earthquake and tornado households who refused further cooperation with the study took more hazard events with them out of the
sample than did the noncooperating victims of the other hazard
types. Thus, the rate of inclusion of events in the mail follow-up
was very high for fire and flood events (over 90% of all reported
fire and flood events were included) and lower for the other three
hazard types.

Among those events included in the initial follow-up sample,
a small percentage (4.7%) were lost because of undeliverable
questionnaire packets. There is not much difference in this percentage across the hazard types, with fire events being the most
likely to be excluded for this reason (6.3%).

Section B of Table 3.2 presents the final disposition rates for
the remaining hazard events that were eligible for the follow-up
sample. This table shows both the percentage of events for which
there was a completed mail questionnaire and those with a completed phone interview. Overall, the completion rate was highest
for fire events (53.5% of all fire questionnaires were completed)
and lowest for tornado events (36.3%). The rate of telephone interviews was much lower than the rate of completed mail questionnaires for all hazard types. Overall, 33.1% of the events had completed mail questionnaires, and only 7.4% of the hazard event
information was obtained by a phone interview.

The differences by type of hazard in the percentage of events
for which a response of "never happened" was given were similar
to those found in the household disposition counts in Table 3.3.
Tornado and earthquake events were more likely to be reported as
having "never happened" (15.9% and 14.3%, respectively) than
were fire events (7.8%).

There are several possible reasons for the appearance of so
many "never happened" responses. First of all, in the telephone
survey an adult was reporting on the experiences of the household; some experiences that occurred to individuals outside the
household context (e.g., at work or while traveling or on vacation)
may have been erroneously included. Second, the telephone interview used the term *experienced* to obtain responses about

whether a hazard incident had occurred in the household. *Experience* may have been interpreted by some to mean the occurrence of the hazard event in the neighborhood, in the community, or in the general vicinity of the respondent household. The mailed questionnaire, in contrast, with its emphasis on injuries and damages may have implied incidents with a more direct impact, with which the experiences of the households in question were clearly poor matches. In addition, the mailed questionnaire emphasized the interest of the study in incidents that had occurred within the household context; hence, events that occurred to persons before they entered the household may have been initially and erroneously reported. In any event, the "never happened" responses were very likely corrected interpretations of the inherently ambiguous questions used in the telephone screening interviews.

The last line of Section B in Table 3.2 shows the overall response rate for the hazard events in the survey, calculated as before for households. Overall, the survey obtained a response for 54.1% of all eligible events, and the response rate was similar for all hazard types (the highest response rate was for fire events: 61.1%).

Summarizing briefly: Households and the hazards they had experienced were lost to our research through any of several mechanisms. A substantial number were lost at the stage of screening, from among households who refused to participate in the screening interview or from among those who did not participate in screening for other reasons. Because we have no additional information on the nonparticipants in the screening interview, no estimate of the ensuing bias can be made. Additional households were lost at the end of screening, because they were among those who declined to participate in the follow-up mail survey. Because screening data are available on these households, some analysis of the nature of these losses at this stage can be undertaken, as shown in the following section.

Among the victimized households that passed through the screening and into the study's second phase, subsequent losses to the sample occurred, again, through several mechanisms. Some "victims" of nondamaging tornadoes, hurricanes, and earthquakes were not included as part of the follow-up sampling strategy discussed above. Because this sampling was done strictly by probability methods, the lost cases at this stage differed from the remaining "no damage" cases only by chance alone, and no further analysis is warranted. Many additional households were, in effect, "lost" because they reported, contrary to the screening information, that their event "never happened." Most of these losses apparently concerned minor events whose *sequelae* failed, on second thought, to qualify them as "disasters" in the respondents' minds. Finally, many cases were lost simply because the eligible respondents, even after repeated pestering, never returned their questionnaires. Again, because we have screening data for each of these households, some analysis of the nature of these losses can also be undertaken.

ANALYSIS OF NONRESPONSE

Refusal to Cooperate after Screening

As we have stated previously, the screening interview located a total of 3,292 hazard-victimized households. Including initial refusals that were eventually converted, 2,603 of these households ultimately cooperated in the study, at least to the extent of providing a name and a mailing address. All told, then, 689 otherwise potentially eligible households (20.9%) were lost to the study through refusing to cooperate further after screening.

The key distinguishing feature of the "refusers" at this stage is that their hazard losses were relatively minor, a pattern that holds across hazard types. Among fire victims (N = 553), for example, 78 reported that the fire they had experienced actually caused no damage; among this group, refusal to cooperate further ran to 29.5%, versus a refusal rate of 10.9% among fire victims who reported any losses (N = 475). For flood victims, the corre-

sponding rates were 27% (N = 89) among those suffering no loss
and 13% (N = 239) among the remainder; for hurricanes, 25.3% (N
= 360) versus 11.6% (N = 303); for tornadoes, 28.3% (N = 637)
versus 13.1% (N = 803); and for earthquakes, 25.9% (N = 851)
versus 22.2% (N = 126). With the partial exception of earthquakes, then, the "refusers" at this stage were similar to the "never happened" category at the stage of the mail questionnaire: Respondents with minor or trivial hazard losses selected themselves
out of the study.

Nonresponse to the Mail Questionnaire

Of the 2,603 households eligible after screening for further
participation, a total of 1,694 ultimately returned one or more of
their questionnaires or, in a few cases, supplied victimization data
over the phone.[3] Thus, between the end of screening and the end
of fieldwork, an additional 909 cases were lost. Of these, 108 were
lost through bad addresses (questionnaires returned to us as "undeliverable"), and the remaining 801 were lost because they simply never returned any questionnaire and were never reached by
telephone (or refused to cooperate).

In order to inquire more fully into the characteristics of—and
the possible biases introduced by—nonresponse to the mail questionnaire, a variable was created that assumed the value 0 for the
801 true nonresponders and the value 1 for the responders. (Note,
then, that the "undeliverables" are excluded from this analysis,
whereas the "never happeneds" are included and treated as responders.) This variable was in turn entered as the dependent
variable in a series of regression equations. The regressors in these
equations included both event characteristics and household
characteristics, and a large number of possible models were estimated. The analysis revealed a few statistically significant effects,

[3]Of these, to be sure, 315 responded with the information that the event "never
happened." These are included as responders in the ensuing analysis, although
they are dropped from most of the substantive analyses of later chapters.

all modest in substantive implications (see Table 3.4). For example, residents of large cities were slightly less likely to respond than residents of rural places; blacks and renters were slightly less likely to respond than whites and homeowners. All these effects,

TABLE 3.4
Regression of Mail Survey Response Status[a] on Hazard
and Household Characteristics

	b	SE
Fire experience	−.002	(.003)
Flood experience	−.015	(.036)
Hurricane experience	−.001	(.029)
Tornado experience	−.001	(.027)
Earthquake experience	−.051	(.030)
Experience of any damage	−.007	(.022)
Total questionnaires sent	−.016*	(.006)
Pacific[b]	−.097	(.053)
Mountain	−.045	(.074)
West North Central	−.050	(.050)
East North Central	−.014	(.043)
West South Central	−.082	(.049)
East South Central	−.042	(.050)
South Atlantic	−.035	(.044)
Middle Atlantic	−.059	(.047)
Large city 250,000+[c]	−.070*	(.035)
Medium city 25,000−250,000	−.015	(.031)
Small town under 25,000	−.012	(.028)
Suburban area	−.030	(.029)
White respondent[d]	.128*	(.039)
Other race (nonblack)	.132	(.070)
Years household in existence from 1970 to 1980	.162	(.036)
Age of head of household	.001	(.001)
Income (in thousands)	.001	(.001)
Homeowner[e]	.069*	(.026)
Constant	.522*	(.072)
$R^2 = .030$		
N = (2,376)		

[a]Response status: 1 = completed questionnaires or "never happened" response; 0 = no response or refused.
[b]Dummy variables for region. Omitted category is New England.
[c]Dummy variables for city size. Omitted category is rural.
[d]Dummy variable for race of respondent. Omitted category is black.
[e]Dummy variable for tenure. Omitted category is renter.
*Significant at .05.

although "significant," are very modest in actual magnitude. There was also a significant tendency for the responses to decline as the number of questionnaires sent increased, as one might expect. About the only important finding to emerge from this set of analyses, however, is that the best fitting model we examined accounted only for 3% of the variance in response. As a substantive conclusion, then, it can be stated that nonresponse to the mail survey was for all practical purposes random with respect to the variables available for analysis.

Nonresponse to the mailed survey represents a loss not only of respondents but also of hazard events. After screening, there remained 2,603 eligible households, representing 3,961 eligible hazard events. (See Table 3.2 for details and definitions of eligibility.) Table 3.5 presents the completion rates within the event samples according to the characteristics of the event. The event information shown here was, of course, obtained from the screener interview and therefore contains little detail. However, the table does allow us to check whether the respondents were more or less likely to respond to questionnaires directed at hazard events of different types.

The first section of the table shows a breakdown of the response rates within the categories of damage. Overall, there is little relationship. In fact, events with large amounts of reported damage ($1,000 or more) were slightly *less* likely to result in a response than were those causing no damage (52.7% vs. 60.2%). However, this pattern varies across the five hazard types. Response to fire events increased with damage, the anticipated pattern. A mixed pattern is found for floods: 47.1% of the no-damage floods and 55.8% of the largest damage floods generated a completed response, but the highest response rate was for floods that caused modest amounts of damage (70.8%). For the remaining three hazards, the tendency was for the response to fall as damage increased. In part, this apparently counterintuitive pattern reflects the fact that "never happened" is treated as a response (vs. a nonresponse) in this table.

The table also shows the response pattern by year of occurrence. The response rates for fires, floods, and hurricanes show

Table 3.5

Percentage of Eligible Events[a] for Which a Response[b] Was Obtained in the Mail Survey by Event Characteristics

	Total	Fire	Flood	Hurricane	Tornado	Earthquake
Total response rate	54.2	61.1	50.5	54.8	52.2	55.3
	(3,961)	(475)	(380)	(622)	(1,581)	(903)
Damage category[c]						
No damage	60.2	51.2	47.1	60.7	59.9	62.2
	(1,323)	(41)	(70)	(196)	(394)	(622)
$1–$100	56.2	57.9	70.8	71.9	55.0	39.5
	(317)	(38)	(24)	(32)	(180)	(43)
$101–$500	49.5	56.8	50.0	52.0	47.3	48.1
	(602)	(74)	(54)	(98)	(349)	(27)
$500–$1,000	56.0	66.0	38.0	59.3	56.0	69.2
	(300)	(53)	(50)	(59)	(125)	(13)
$1,000 or more	52.7	63.6	55.8	43.9	50.4	30.2
	(729)	(217)	(113)	(114)	(232)	(53)
Unknown	47.0	61.5	47.8	51.2	46.2	39.3
	(690)	(52)	(69)	(123)	(301)	(145)
Year of occurrence[c]						
1970–1975	50.6	61.7	50.0	51.1	48.9	45.8
	(1,250)	(180)	(164)	(176)	(468)	(262)
1976–1980	55.7	61.0	50.5	55.6	53.4	59.0
	(2,449)	(277)	(200)	(383)	(1,016)	(573)
Unknown	58.0	55.6	56.3	60.3	55.7	60.3
	(262)	(18)	(16)	(63)	(97)	(68)

[a]Percentages based on "eligible events" excluding noncooperation and undelivered questionnaires. See Table 3.2.
[b]Response includes completed questionnaires and "never happened."
[c]Data obtained from screener interview.

very little difference by year. The pattern for tornadoes and, more strongly, for earthquakes shows higher response rates for more recent events, as might be expected, given the high proportion of "trivials" in these two categories.

Sample Characteristics

Net of all losses, there were in the end 13,005 households that completed the screening interview and 1,379 households who eventually supplied follow-up data on hazard victimization, this latter number *excluding* the respondents in the "never happened" category. These are, in essence, the samples available for (1) es-

TABLE 3.6
Sociodemographic Characteristics of the Screener and Follow-Up Samples

	Screener sample	Mail sample
Sex		
Male (%)	38.5	39.1
Female (%)	61.5	60.9
N =	(13,005)	(1,379)
Race		
White (%)	89.4	91.5
Black (%)	7.6	5.4
Other (%)	3.0	3.1
N =	(12,608)	(1,371)
Tenure		
Own (%)	74.7	77.5
Rent (%)	25.3	21.8
N =	(12,589)	(1,379)
Community size		
Rural (%)	21.3	23.3
Small town under 25,000 (%)	26.7	25.3
Suburb of city 25,000+ (%)	22.8	23.6
Medium city 25,000–250,000 (%)	16.4	17.0
Large city 250,000+ (%)	12.6	10.5
Other (%)	0.2	0.3
N =	(12,517)	(1,369)
Age of head of household		
Under 25 (%)	6.0	7.1
25–34 (%)	23.4	28.6
35–44 (%)	20.4	25.5
45–54 (%)	17.7	17.5
55–64 (%)	16.2	12.8
65+ (%)	16.4	8.6
N =	(12,295)	(1,356)
Average age	46.3	42.8
Family income		
Average family income (1979)	$18,503	$20,876
N =	(11,008)	(1,275)
Number of persons in household		
Average household size	3.0	3.3
N =	(12,520)	(1,347)

timating the rates of victimization by natural hazard in the United States (the final screener sample), and (2) estimating the average losses, insurance coverage, relief assistance, and so on of hazard victims (the final mail-survey sample, net of the "never happened" group). Some basic descriptive data on these two samples are shown in Table 3.6.

If we focus first on the screener interview, we note a fairly large "bias" in favor of female respondents. Because households are the unit of analysis for this research, and any adult was treated as an eligible informant for the household as a whole, the screening interviews were conducted with any adult who happened to be present in the household when contact was made. The differential tendency of women to be in the home, relative to men, at any given time thus accounts for the indicated pattern. Note that women were also more likely than men to fill out the mail questionnaire, presumably because the name of the phone respondent was used on the mailing label.

The remaining distributions, for both the mail and the screener samples, are about as one would expect, given the known demographic characteristics of the U.S. population; all the reported proportions are within a few percentage points of the correct values. Note that differences *between* the two samples can arise in either of two ways: (1) because of correlated nonresponse to the mail follow-up (i.e., certain classes of respondents may have been more hesitant than others to return their questionnaires), or (2) because some groups in the society are more vulnerable to victimization by hazards than others. In general, however, the distributions reported for the two samples are quite similar, which suggests that neither of the above processes was at work.

SUMMARY

The design of the household victimization study consisted of data gathered in two stages: a telephone screening interview of a large number of U.S. households and a follow-up mail question-naire. The screening interview for the first part of the study was based on a random sample of all telephone-owning U.S. house-holds drawn with a random-digit-dialing sampling technique. A total of 13,005 phone interviews were completed for a response rate of 63.5% of all contacted, eligible households. Of this group, 3,292 households (or 25%) reported one or more hazard experi-ences from 1970 to 1980 for a total of 6,177 discrete disaster events.

The follow-up questionnaires were mailed to the 2,603 households in which the respondents agreed to cooperate in the study. At the completion of the fieldwork, a total of 1,694 house-holds had responded with completed mail or phone interviews ($N = 1,379$) or by indicating that the specified hazard had never occurred or was too trivial ($N = 315$). A total of 1,603 event ques-tionnaires, then, formed the final sample for the second stage of the study.

The data gathered from the initial phone screening interview allowed for an analysis of the possible biases produced through nonresponse to the various stages of the fieldwork. We found some tendency for respondents who reported no damage from the disaster to refuse the mail survey (either by refusing to cooperate and provide an address or by later reporting that the hazard never occurred). Thus, some of the more minor disasters were self-se-lected out of the study. Among the households that received a questionnaire, there were few household or disaster characteris-tics related to the probability of a response; the number of ques-tionnaires received, households in large cities, blacks, and renters were negatively related to response, although these effects were small.

CHAPTER 4

The Incidence of Hazard Experiences

INTRODUCTION

How many households are victimized by natural hazard events? What kinds of households are especially likely to have such experiences? These are the two main topics of this chapter. To provide a calibrating framework for natural hazard phenomena—floods, hurricanes, tornadoes, and earthquakes—we compared the incidence of such events with household fires and with other unpleasant occurrences.

Whether a household had experienced any one of the happenings about which we were concerned was subject to some degree of ambiguity. A household fire was perhaps best defined because only those fires that occurred in a dwelling qualified. But there were ambiguous fires: Should a flare-up of grease while cooking be counted? Or a cigarette burn on a rug? Floods were also subject to some ambiguity: If a river overflows its banks and waters swirl around the second story of one's home, there is no doubt that a flood event has occurred. But what about a storm-drain backup in the basement caused by heavy rains? Even more ambiguous are hurricanes, tornadoes, and earthquakes. The direct path of a tornado is usually quite narrow, but dwellings near the path are also often affected by accompanying high winds and torrential

47

rains. Hurricanes cover even wider areas and set off secondary effects such as tornadoes and floods. Earthquakes are similar to hurricanes in not having very definite boundaries of impact. (Indeed, while this chapter was being written, an earthquake of magnitude Richter 4.8 and with an epicenter some 300 miles away was felt as a slight tremor in Amherst, Massachusetts. Certainly a tremor was "experienced" by the authors, and several million others in New England, but scarcely at a level of intensity that endangered life or property.)

The inherent ambiguity of natural hazard experiences was resolved in our questionnaire design by deciding to include at the first level of measurement any event that was regarded by a household as an "experience" with any of the hazards under study. These hazard experiences would then be filtered through a series of questions that would separate out the trivial (and remote) experiences from those with serious consequences and a direct immediate impact. The question used in our telephone interviews was worded as follows: "Since 1970, has your family or household experienced a [hazard] in a house or apartment in which you were living as a group?" The hazards were described as follows:

"a fire"
"a flood caused by the overflowing of a river or stream"
"a hurricane or severe tropical storm"
"a tornado or severe windstorm"
"an earthquake or tremor"

The intent of the question was to focus the attention of the respondent on a specific period (1970 through 1980) and on events that occurred in or around a dwelling unit occupied by the group of persons who then currently constituted a household or living group. How successful these questions were in focusing the respondent's attention on that period or on the specific household, as intended, is a matter of speculation. Our main safeguard against errors were follow-up questions that asked about specific dates of occurrences and about the length of time the household in question had been in existence.

Of course, this strategy left it completely up to the respondent to define a hazard "experience." We assume that most respondents used low thresholds in reporting on experiences. Indeed, as we show later in this chapter, that assumption is justified.

The next stage of the filtering process was to ask in which year during the 1970–1980 period the event was experienced. A few persons (5.0%) could not remember dates of occurrence, and no further filtering questions were asked of them.

The second-stage filter was a series of questions asking whether deaths, injuries, and/or damages were experienced as a consequence of the event. As we indicate later, many of the experiences were apparently quite trivial events; at least, no one in the household was hurt and no household property was damaged.

The term *hazard experience* is used in this chapter to designate all the reports received from our respondents in response to the first question listed above, less those events for which they could not provide a date. A hazard experience, then, is the most inclusive category of measurement, including all those happenings for which the respondent could provide a year of occurrence and that appeared to the respondent to have been a household fire, flood, hurricane, tornado, or earthquake (irrespective of loss). Later, we distinguished between *experience* and *victimization*, the latter being any experience in which some loss was incurred.

THE BASE PERIOD AND ITS REPRESENTATIVENESS

The incidence rates to be presented in this chapter are tied to the particular base period used: the 11 years contained in 1970 through 1980. The rates computed are historically specific and may not be representative of incidence rates computed over different periods or longer ranges of time. This potential unrepresentativeness is particularly troublesome for those hazards and for hazard magnitudes that have long or irregular return cycles. Thus, the incidence of household fires does not vary much from year to year and from decade to decade. The household fire rates computed are therefore likely to be typical of any 11-year period. But major earthquakes have longer return cycles, and hence, our findings about that hazard are likely to be specific to a historical period in which only one major earthquake occurred, the San Fernando tremor of 1971, and that event was scarcely a major catastrophe. Similarly, the floods spawned by Hurricane Agnes in 1972 were the ordinary *sequelae* not of a severe tropical storm, but only of one that turned into heavy rainstorms when it left the coast and veered inland.

There is simply no way that we can claim with complete confidence that the period under study is clearly representative of all historical periods and all future periods. The best we can say is that 1970–1980 is not totally misleading for fires, tornadoes, and floods. However, one should take our findings with respect to earthquakes with due regard for the fact that during the period in question, no serious earthquake catastrophe occurred. With respect to hurricanes, the appearance of Agnes in the time window affects our findings to some extent.

Of course, the same cautions should be exercised when we consider the traces of public policy effects shown in Chapter 6. A major change in federal policies affecting relief and rehabilitation measures occurred with the passage of PL93-288 in 1974. In addition, the National Flood Insurance Program began to get under way in earnestness during the last few years of this period. Whatever traces we see of the actions of federal agencies is therefore reflected in the patterns of aid claimed by the households studied, which arose out of several major policy shifts that occurred during this period.

In short, our findings are historically specific, as the findings for an 11-year period in the past and future would be.

HAZARD EXPERIENCES

The percentages of the 13,005 households contacted during screening that claimed hazard experiences of any magnitude are

TABLE 4.1

All Hazard Experiences[a] Reported by Respondents from 1970 to 1980
(N = 13,005)

Hazard Type	Percentage reporting any experience[a] (1970–1980)	Any experience[a] annual rate per 1,000 households[b]	Projected U.S. households all experience[a,c] (annual)
Household fires	4.3	6.8	544,000
Floods	2.5	4.4	352,000
Hurricanes or severe tropical storms	5.1	8.2	656,000
Tornadoes or severe windstorms	11.1	18.2	1,455,000
Earthquakes or tremors	7.5	13.7	1,095,000
All hazard experiences combined	25.3	51.2	4,093,000

[a]Includes any report of each hazard, regardless of seriousness of incident. Does not count separately multiple incidents occurring within any year or over the period. Includes any event reported at any time during 1970 through 1980.
[b]Computed by considering as base only households that had been formed at the time of the incident.
[c]Based on U.S. Census 1980 count of 79,951,490 households in continental contiguous states (excludes Hawaii and Alaska), rounded to nearest thousand.

shown in the first column of Table 4.1. Even under our rather lenient and inclusive definitions, hazard experiences were relatively rare. During the 11-year period, 4.3% experienced a household fire, 2.5% a flood, 5.1% a hurricane (or severe tropical storm), 11.1% a tornado (or severe windstorm), and 7.5% an earthquake (or tremor). All told, a little more than one in every four households (25.3%) experienced at least one of the five hazards in that period.[1]

In the second column of Table 4.1, we have converted the

[1]Households experiencing more than one hazard or several instances of the same hazard are counted only once in this calculation.

reported experiences into rates per 1,000 households per year, a calculation that takes into account the fact that some of the households in the sample had been formed sometime during the 11-year period and hence were not exposed to risk during the entire period.[2] Annual "experience" rates per 1,000 households ranged from a low of 4.4 for floods to a high of 18.2 for tornadoes and severe windstorms. All told, about 1 out of 20 households can be expected to experience one or another of the five hazards during a typical year.

The third column of Table 4.1 projects the total expected numbers of U.S. households who will experience each of the five hazards annually, assuming that the 11 years, 1970–1980, provide an adequate basis for such projections. About 4 million U.S. households will have at least one experience in a year, about half of such events consisting of earthquake tremors and tornadoes (including windstorms).

HAZARD VICTIMIZATION EXPERIENCES

At the level of hazard experiences, natural hazards appear to be quite frequent, experienced by about one-quarter of all households in an average decade. But this definition, of course, includes many events of only momentary consequence (e.g., events not accompanied by any damage to property or injury to household members). For policy purposes, then, the definition of hazard experience is overinclusive, as Table 4.2 shows. In that table, the proportions of experiences involving deaths, injuries, or any damages are shown. The bottom row shows that most of the

[2]Rates were calculated as follows:

$$\text{Rate} = (\sum_{i}^{N} H_i/Y_i) \times 1,000$$

where H_i = number of hazard events reported by individual i.
Y_i = number of years during the period 1970–1980 the household of individual i was in existence.
N = total sample (13,005).

TABLE 4.2
Deaths, Injuries, and Damages from Natural Hazard Events

Natural hazard type	Deaths		Injuries[a]		Damages[b]		Deaths, and/or injuries and/or damages	N of households reporting any experience of each type[c]
	N	Percent	N	Percent	N	Percent	Percent	
Fires	(17)	3.1	(39)	7.1	(475)	85.9	85.9	(553)
Floods	(7)	2.1	(9)	2.7	(239)	72.9	73.2	(328)
Hurricanes	(2)	0.3	(4)	0.6	(303)	45.7	46.0	(663)
Tornadoes	(8)	0.6	(14)	1.0	(803)	55.8	56.0	(1,440)
Earthquakes	(9)	0.9	(7)	0.7	(126)	12.9	13.6	(977)
All hazard types combined	(43)	1.3	(73)	2.2	(1,946)	59.1	60.8	(3,292)[d]

[a]Any injuries reported.
[b]Any damages, regardless of amount or extent.
[c]Number of households reporting each hazard type. Actual separate incidents within each hazard type are not counted as individual incidents.
[d]Number of hazard types combined reported by households, not counting separate events within each type.

events reported were fairly trivial occurrences: memorable enough to report, to be sure, but with minimally serious or nonexistent consequences in the way of injuries or property damage. Indeed, nearly two-fifths of the experiences reported (39.2%) were trivial events, in the above sense.[3]

As the table shows, there are sharp differences across hazards types in the proportions of "trivial" events reported. The fire experiences captured by our methods were least likely to be trivial events: About 86% of the reported incidents were accompanied by some injuries and/or damages. The same was true in a lesser degree for floods: 73% of the flood events in the sample inflicted at least some damage. In contrast, geographically diffuse natural hazard experiences with earthquakes and hurricanes were most likely to be trivial events (86.4% and 54.0%, respectively, being accompanied by no injuries or damages). Tornadoes and windstorms occupied a middle ground, with 44.0% classifiable as trivial events, in our terms.

When we narrow the definition of hazard events to include only hazard victimization experiences, as in Table 4.3, the overall incidence declines considerably. In the sense used in this table, a *hazard victimization experience* is one that is accompanied by death and/or injury and/or nonzero damage to property. Of course, because injuries and deaths are relatively rare (as Table

---

[3]To prevent misunderstanding, a *trivial* hazard experience is here taken to mean an experience reported by a household that did not result in death or injury to any member *of that household* and that did not generate any damage to the household property. This is a narrow definition of *trivial*. To illustrate, consider a family that resided on the outskirts of a major tornado path. The tornado itself may well have destroyed hundreds of homes and injured scores of people. If our hypothetical family escaped unscathed, incurring no injuries or loss *themselves*, the "event" is counted here as a trivial one, even though the tornado itself clearly was not. (It must, of course, be remembered that the households directly in the path would have been equally likely to appear in our victim sample.) Also, from a psychological viewpoint, the above "experience" would in all likelihood not have been trivial, even in the absence of direct losses to the reporting households. On the contrary, it may well have been the most awesome and terrifying event in the whole of their existence.

TABLE 4.3

Hazard Victimization Experiences[a] Reported by Respondents from 1970 to 1980 (N = 12,352)[b]

Hazard type	Percentage reporting hazard victimization experience[a]	Victimization experience[a] annual rate per 1,000 households[c]	Projected U.S. households with victimization experiences[a] (annual)
Fires	3.8	5.8	464,000
Floods	1.9	3.4	272,000
Hurricanes and severe tropical storms	2.5	3.5	272,000
Tornadoes and severe windstorms	6.5	10.0	799,510
Earthquakes and tremors	1.1	1.8	138,000
All hazard victimization experiences combined	14.3	24.5	1,959,000

[a]A hazard victimization experience is defined as one involving death, and/or injury, and/or damage to property.
[b]Excludes households that could not recall year of occurrence or that, by error, were not asked follow-up questions on injuries, deaths, or damages.
[c]Standardized by number of years households had been in existence during 1970–1980.

4.2 indicates), most of the hazard victimization experiences were ones that caused some damage to property and/or possessions.

Table 4.3 shows that when we consider only hazard victimization experiences (or, in other words, nontrivial hazard events), the incidence proportions and rates decline, on the average, to about half the size of the corresponding numbers in Table 4.1.

About 14% of the households surveyed experienced some hazard victimization event in the 11-year period, equivalent to a rate of slightly less than 25 households out of 1,000 in any year. Projected to the total household population of the contiguous 48 states, about 2 million households annually experience one or another of these five events with resulting damage and/or injury.

Note that this definition of *nontrivial* can easily be regarded as very much on the lenient side. Although the respondents claimed some damage, the amount of damages involved may have been quite small. Indeed, as we show in the next chapter, many of the nontrivial experiences counted in Table 4.3 were not very different from the trivial ones that we have excluded from that table.

Among the hazards studied, tornado and windstorm victimization experiences were easily the most frequent, with annual rates of 10.00 per 1,000 households. Because the best documentary records indicate a considerably lower incidence of damage and injuries for tornadoes alone,[4] we suspect that many of the incidents reported were windstorms without accompanying tornado activity. Household fire victimizations were next in terms of frequency, with annual rates of 5.8 per 1,000 households. Hurricanes and floods had about the same victimization incidence levels: 3.5 and 3.4 per 1,000, respectively. Least frequent of all were reports of earthquake victimization events, with annual rates of 1.8 per 1,000.

By and large, households experienced only one type of hazard victimization event throughout the 1970–1980 period. Table 4.4 indicates that about 13.6% of all the sampled households ex-

[4]See section later in this chapter for comparisons with other estimates.

TABLE 4.4

Multiple Victimization Experiences with Natural Hazards, 1970–1980

Number of hazard victimization experiences of any type

Number of event years	Percentage
0	86.4
1	12.3
2	1.2
3 or 4[a]	0.1
	N = (13,005)

Pairwise overlapping of hazard victimization experiences

		Floods	Hurricanes	Tornadoes	Earthquakes
Fires	%	0.17[b]	0.15	0.35	0.06
	N	(22)	(20)	(45)	(8)
Floods	%		0.18	0.22	0.03
	N		(23)	(29)	(4)
Hurricanes	%			0.30	0.02
	N			(39)	(3)
Tornadoes	%				0.07
	N				(9)

[a]Only one household reported four victimization incidents.
[b]Percentage of total sample ($N = 13,005$) experiencing both fire and flood victimization experiences. Number in brackets is number of households with that joint experience.

perienced one or more hazard victimizations, of which 12.3% experienced only one hazard victimization between 1970 and 1980.[5] Only a very small proportion experienced two or more (1.3%) and only one household experienced four nontrivial hazard types. None experienced more than four hazard types.

The bottom section of Table 4.4 presents counts of the joint occurrence of pairs of hazard victimization. Not very much can be

[5]Note that this table is based on the total sample, 13,005, and includes those who were not able to remember the year in which a reported hazard occurred. Table 4.3 excludes the latter and hence reports a slightly higher proportion reporting a hazard victimization event (14.3%). Note also that this tabulation counts as a single event all separate occurrences of a natural hazard type that took place within a calendar year. Because very few households experienced multiple occurrences of a given disaster type within a year, this mode of presentation does not seriously distort reality.

noted in this display: Joint experiences of different types of non-trivial natural hazards events over the 1970–1980 period were quite rare. Indeed, although there is a slight tendency for all the events to be slightly positively related, these patterns are so weak as to be insignificant substantively and statistically.

Comparisons with Other Estimates

In order to design the research that is discussed in this monograph, it was necessary to assemble as much as possible of the existing information on household victimization by hazards. Indeed, it was existing data on which we based the size of the screening-interview sample and calculated the costs of contacting impacted households by mail. The resulting design estimates are shown in Table 4.5. (Appendix A provides a detailed account of how these estimates were constructed.)

Because several sources of existing data were consulted, the estimates of victimizations per decade varied slightly depending on which source was used. The American National Red Cross Chapter Reports (filed by chapters after rendering aid in disaster events) tended to be concerned with disasters of relatively wide scope, and hence, they undercounted impacted households when only a few were involved. Surveys conducted by the senior authors in California and among political elites in a sample of states and local communities asked respondents about lifetime experiences and hence produced overestimates, especially as the questions eliciting victimization reports used the term *experienced*, as in the screening interview. Hence "high" and "low" estimates were calculated. The "design" estimate shown in the third column of Table 4.5 contains the "compromise guesses" on which the size of the screening sample was based.

Note that the design estimates are close to the hazard victimization findings, as reported in the last column of Table 4.5, but that they depart considerably from the "hazard experiences" reported (i.e., the total of nontrivial and trivial hazard reports), es-

TABLE 4.5

Ex Ante and Ex Post Hazard Victimization Estimates for U.S. Households[c] (Percentages)

Hazard types	Ex Ante estimates			Ex Post decade estimates	
	High estimate	Low estimate	Design[d] estimate	Hazard experiences reported	Hazard victimization only
Fires[a]	5	1.0	4	4.3	3.8
Floods[b]	4	1.1	3	2.5	1.9
Hurricanes[b]	5	1.5	3	5.1	2.5
Tornadoes[b]	2	0.3	1	11.1	6.5
Earthquakes[b]	0.7	0.01	0.5	7.5	1.1
Combined			14.5	25.3	14.3

[a]Based on data gathered in a household survey in selected California communities, plus data gathered in a survey of state and local political elites (see Rossi and Wright, 1982, for detailed discussion of these data). In addition, survey data gathered by the National Fire Prevention and Control Administration (National Household Fire Survey, 1977) and compilations of the chapter reports of the American National Red Cross were consulted.
[b]Based on data from the chapter reports of the American National Red Cross plus the two surveys cited in footnote *a* above.
[c]See Appendix A, in which these estimates are derived in detail.
[d]"Design estimate" is a compromise between the high and low estimates used in the design of the victimization-study sampling-strategy.

pecially for tornadoes and earthquakes (the two hazards for which many trivial events were reported). Because the sources on which the design estimates were based counted mainly what were thought to be household victimizations, we find the correspondence to be comforting.

The design estimates and the actual findings concerning hazard victimizations do depart in significant ways, however. The design estimates lead one to expect more flood victimizations than the sample reported (3% as compared with 1.9%) and considerably fewer tornado or windstorm victimizations than the sampled households reported. We have no easy explanation for the differences between the two flood estimates, except to question whether the "compromise" should have been centered as close to the "high" estimate. We suspect that the discrepancy between design and findings for tornadoes occurred because we added "severe windstorms" to the tornado category in the screening interview, whereas the design estimates were based on events that were limited to tornadoes alone.

YEAR-BY-YEAR HAZARD VICTIMIZATION RATES, 1970 THROUGH 1980

Table 4.6 contains annual hazard victimization rates (per 1,000 households) year by year for the 1970–80 period. Although 1980 was not a particularly hazardous year, the highest overall annual rate was recorded for that year, largely reflecting the high rate that year of tornadoes and windstorms (14.77). Note also that there appears to have been a trend through the 11-year period for the combined overall annual rate to increase. We suspect that this increase is due to the "telescoping" effect noted in several similar

TABLE 4.6
Annual Hazard Victimization Rates (1970 through 1980): Incidents per 1,000 Households[a]

Year	Fires	Floods	Hurricanes	Tornadoes	Earthquakes	Combined serious hazards
1970	2.39	1.02	1.14	3.41	1.02	8.97
1971	1.71	0.88	0.77	2.97	3.74	10.12
1972	3.05	5.69	1.90	4.21	1.47	16.32
1973	2.84	1.83	1.83	4.67	0.20	11.47
1974	4.21	1.08	1.37	5.88	0.29	12.83
1975	4.03	1.31	1.69	4.97	0.28	12.29
1976	4.26	1.90	2.08	5.07	0.09	13.41
1977	3.92	2.44	2.18	7.23	0.44	16.20
1978	4.90	3.49	3.49	8.22	0.25	18.84
1979	4.79	2.07	6.30	9.18	0.88	23.22
1980	4.38	2.46	4.15	14.77	1.85	27.60

[a]Considers only victimization incidents (involving deaths, injuries, or damages). Rates computed by considering only households in existence in the year in question.

investigations.[6] Events that occurred sometime ago tended to be recalled as happening more recently. Thus, the reports of natural hazard events in the later years of the period may actually refer to ones that took place much earlier.

Year-to-year fluctuations in the rates are also of interest. Some reflect the occurrence of fairly large-scale hazard events. For example, the high rate for floods in 1972 is consistent with the severe flooding of the valleys of the Susquehanna as a consequence of that year's Hurricane Agnes. Similarly, the high earthquake rate for 1971 coincides with the San Fernando quake of that year, and the high rate for 1980 coincides with the Ohio Valley shocks of that year.

These findings suggest that the recall methods used in the screening interview did not lead to perfectly precise and accurate locating of even nontrivial hazard events in time.[7]

MULTIPLE NATURAL-HAZARD VICTIMIZATION-EVENTS

The data shown in Table 4.3 provide one way of answering the question of how important natural hazard events are. The answer given there is that victimizations by floods, hurricanes, and earthquakes were, at least for this period, less frequently encountered than household fires. Table 4.3 also indicates that tor-

---

[6]This telescoping effect is even more severe if we consider the trivial hazard events as well as the ones reported in Table 4.6. Combined victimization and trivial annual rates show an even stronger tendency toward an apparent increase toward the end of the 11-year period. Because victimizations are more likely to be remembered in sharper detail, we would expect trivial ones to be more likely to be telescoped.   .

[7]The "telescoping" of hazard events into proximate years makes it difficult to produce annualized rates that do not artificially enhance the incidence of hazards among newly formed households. Because such newly formed households have been in existence for a short time, the telescoped events reported by them lead to artificially enhanced rates of occurrence. Hence, in the remainder of the chapter, we consider whether or not a household reported an experience with at least one serious hazard event (of each type) as the basic measure of hazard incidence.

nadoes and windstorms were a bit more than two-thirds more frequent than fires.

It is important to note that our measures of incidence center on whether a household has had *any* victimization encounter with a hazard of a given type. Thus, a household that had only one fire victimization within the 1970–1980 period is regarded as having had a nontrivial encounter. Households that have had more than one victimization are treated identically to those with a single encounter.

Because of a technical error in drafting the screening interview, we did not ask death, injury, and damage questions separately for each hazard event that occurred within a single year. Hence, although we were able to tabulate the number of separate hazard events that were claimed as experiences by the respondents, we could not separate the trivial from the nontrivial within any given year of multiple events. Table 4.7 contains the counts of all separate events—trivial and nontrivial—that were reported by the respondents. Note that it was precisely from the hazard types that are likely to contain many trivial occurrences—tornadoes and earthquakes—that most of the multiple within-year reports were obtained. The main message of Table 4.7 is that households reporting a hazard experience as occurring during the 1970–1980 period overwhelmingly reported only one such occurrence. However, the range is considerable. One respondent reported 110 tornado–windstorm events during the decade, and another reported 33 earthquake–tremor experiences.[8] It is a safe guess that most of these multiple reportings were of trivial events.

In any event, because of the impossibility of sorting out the trivial experiences from victimizations year by year in the data

---

[8]These maxima are artificially precise. In the interview protocol, allowance was made for up to 10 events to be reported in any single year. There were 11 years asked about. Thus, by construction, the maximum number of events of any type that could be reported for the base period was 10 × 11 = 110. In like fashion, the report of "33 earthquake or tremor" events over the base period was derived from a response of "Oh, there must have been about three a year," multiplied by the 11 years.

TABLE 4.7

Numbers of Event Years, Separate Events, and Event Incidence Rates (Trivial and Victimization Incidents Combined)

Household fires

Years with fires	Percent	Number of fires	Percent	
0	95.75	0	95.75	Incidence of separate fires per decade per 1,000 households: 7.328
1	4.14	1	4.06	Number of separate fires reported in sample: 586
2	.10	2	.16	
3	.01	3–6	.03	
Average	.044	Average	.045	

Floods

Years with floods	Percent	Number of floods	Percent	
0	97.48	0	97.48	Separate flood events per decade per 1,000 households: 6.114
1	2.28	1	2.04	Number of separate flood events reported in sample: 483
2	.18	2	.32	
3–11	.05	3–12	.16	
Average	.030	Average	.037	

Hurricanes

Years with hurricanes	Percent	Number of hurricanes	Percent	
0	94.90	0	94.90	Separate hurricane events per decade per 1,000 households: 11.487
1	4.62	1	4.22	Number of separate hurricane events reported: 946
2	.37	2	.49	
3–11	.11	3–4	.25	
		5–20	.14	
Average	.060	Average	.073	

Tornadoes

Years with tornadoes	Percent	Number of tornadoes	Percent	
0	88.93	0	88.93	Separate tornadoes per decade per 1,000 households: 30.917

(continued)

Table 4.7 (Continued)

	Percent		Percent	
1	10.28	1	8.73	Number of separate tornado events reported: 2,501
2–3	.55	2–5	1.90	
4–11	.25	5–11	.40	
		12+	.12	
Average	.136	Average	.200	
Earthquakes				
Years with Earthquakes	Percent	Number of Earthquakes	Percent	Separate earthquake reports per decade per 1,000 households: 21.917
0	92.49	0	92.49	Number of separate earthquake reports: 1,601
1	7.03	1	5.87	
2	.32	2	.78	
3–11	.16	3–5	.62	
		6–33	.25	
Average	.087	Average	.123	
Combined hazards				
Years with hazard reports	Percent	Number of hazard reports	Percent	Separate hazard reports per decade per 1,000 households: 77.763
0	74.69	0	74.69	Number of separate hazard reports: 6,217
1	19.53	1	17.02	
2	4.24	2	4.74	
3	.85	3	1.55	
4–13	.70	4–13	1.70	
		14+	.21	
Average	.356	Average	.478	

obtained from the screening interview, the remainder of the chapter focuses primarily on what might be called the *victimization-year*. That is, we count as a single occurrence a report of one or more hazard victimization events occurring within a year.

Calibrating Natural Hazard Incidence

In order to develop an appreciation of the comparative importance of hazard victimizations, it is useful to compare how frequently other unpleasant experiences occur. In order to provide such comparisons, we asked a subsample (1 household in 10) whether each of 17 unpleasant events had happened to someone in the household during the 1970–1980 period.[9] A tabulation of those unpleasant experiences is shown in Table 4.8.

Because the unpleasant experiences (noxious events) are tabulated in Table 4.8 as incidents of all sorts, trivial and serious combined, the appropriate comparisons are with the five hazard percentages shown in Table 4.1.

The noxious events have been grouped in Table 4.8 according to whether they refer to natural hazards, "bad-luck" events (events over which households had little control), and "personal breakdowns" (events toward the occurrence of which the households and/or an individual may have made some contribution). Hailstorms and severe snowstorms were the two natural hazard

[9]The exact wording of the question was as follows: "Now I will read you a list of acts of nature or other serious events that sometimes happen to people. For each event, please tell me whether or not your family or household has had any experiences of that sort since 1970." For persons who claimed that an event happened to them or their households, a follow-up question asked, "Were there damages or injuries?" This follow-up was asked only for events in which damages or injuries were not obvious consequences (e.g., we regarded unemployment as carrying obvious consequences). The 17 "noxious" events were chosen somewhat arbitrarily: The natural hazards were chosen because the ones in question are frequently referred to as important natural-hazard dangers in the United States; the others were chosen by the research staff as relatively serious events that were alleged to be fairly frequent household experiences.

TABLE 4.8
Selected Other Noxious Events Experienced[a] during Period of
1970–1980 (N = 1,245)

Event	Percentage experienced	Percentage of experiences with damage and/or injury		
		N	Percent	N of events
Other natural hazard events				
Lightning	6.0	(39)	52	(75)
Landslides	0.5	(2)	33	(6)
Hailstorms	11.3	(66)	47	(141)
Snowstorms	37.4	(39)	8	(466)
Ground subsidence	2.7	(3)	9	(34)
"Bad-luck" events				
Auto accident	8.2	(85)	83	(102)
Victim of crime	14.5	(65)	36	(180)
Victim of shooting	0.6	(5)	71	(7)
Unemployment (6 or more months)	13.0	—[b]		—[b]
Birth of defective child	2.3	—		—
Unexpected death of family member	8.8	—		—
Personal breakdowns				
Arrests and imprisonments	1.5	(2)	10	(19)
Drug or alcohol addiction	1.0	(3)	23	(13)
Mental depression	3.8	—		—
Child in trouble	4.0	—		—
Marital breakup	8.7	—		—
Personal bankruptcy	1.4	—		—

[a]Asked only of a 1-in-10 subsample of those given the screening interview.
[b]Questions on damages or injuries not asked about noxious events marked by —.

events that were very frequent, the latter being more frequent than any of the natural hazard events studied in detail in this survey. Lightning strikes appear to have been about as common as household fires, with landslides being more rare than any of the five, and ground subsidence being somewhat rarer still. Of course, the seriousness of the natural hazard events shown in Table 4.8 is somewhat uncertain. On the one hand, about half of the lightning

TABLE 4.9
Incidence Rates for Noxious Events Compared with Natural Hazard Experiences (N = 1,245)

	Annual rates[a] per 1,000 households
All five trivial and nontrivial natural hazards (fires, floods, etc.)	48.3
Other natural hazard events (lightning, snowstorms, etc.)	99.6
Bad-luck events	90.6
Personal breakdown events	42.4
All noxious events	232.6

[a]Computed by adding up the events that occurred in each category and dividing by the number of years the households were exposed to risk.

strikes produced injuries and/or damages, but only 8% of the snowstorms and 9% of the ground subsidences had such effects.

The incidence of "bad-luck" events appears to have been of about the order of the five main hazard experiences. Unemployment lasting six or more months struck about as frequently as hurricane experiences and victimization by crime. Unexpected deaths and serious auto accidents appear to have been about as frequent as earthquake–tremor experiences. Few households were victims of shootings, and few suffered the misfortune of the birth of a defective child.

Most of the personal breakdown events were more rare than any of the five hazards, the main exception being marital disruptions, experienced by a little less than 9% of the households.

Another way of presenting these materials is shown in Table 4.9, which contains annual incidence rates per 1,000 households.[10] The annualized rate for the other natural hazards combined was about twice that for the main five hazards combined, a

[10]Note that the annual incidence rates for the five natural hazards differ from those presented in Table 4.1 (48.3 vs. 51.5) because they were computed only for the 1-in-10 subsample who were asked the noxious events questions.

TABLE 4.10
Noxious Events and Natural Hazard Experiences Compared
(Percentage Reporting at Least One Event)

Noxious events that happened more often than the five natural hazards	
Severe snowstorms	(37.4)
Severe hailstorms	(11.3)
Victimization by crime	(14.5)
Unemployment for six months or more	(13.0)
Noxious events that happened less often than the five natural hazards	
Landslides or cave-ins	(0.5)
Drug or alcohol addiction	(1.0)
Arrest or imprisonment	(1.5)
Being victim of shooting	(0.5)
Birth of a defective child	(2.3)
Personal bankruptcy	(1.4)
Ground subsidence	(2.7)
Noxious events that were as frequent as five natural hazards	
Lightning strikes	(6.0)
Auto accidents	(8.2)
Mental depression	(3.8)
Unexpected family death	(8.8)
Marital disruption	(8.7)

comparison that means that severe snowstorms and hailstorms are more likely to occur than any of the five main natural hazards.

But so were "bad-luck" events more likely than the five natural hazards to occur as a combined set. Only personal breakdowns as a group were less frequently encountered than the five hazards of main interest.

In more specific terms, Table 4.10 groups the noxious events studied into those that occurred more often than the five natural hazards under study, those that occurred less frequently, and finally those that occurred about as often. The five natural hazard experiences (trivial and nontrivial) are thus seen to be on about the same order of magnitude as lightning strikes, auto accidents, mental depression, unexpected family deaths, and marital disruptions.

THE SPATIAL AND SOCIAL DISTRIBUTION OF NATURAL DISASTER EVENTS

Natural hazard events have definite ecological distributions. The paths of hurricanes that impact the continental United States are more likely to strike the Gulf States and the lower Atlantic seaboard. Interior states may sometimes be affected by flooding accompanying heavy rainfall, as in the case of the 1972 Agnes-caused flooding in Pennsylvania, upper New York, and Maryland. Tornadoes are known to favor a diagonal belt running from the Southwest to the Northeast. Earthquakes are more likely to occur along the known fault lines. Floods are less specialized—even the arid states are subject to flash flooding—and all states are subject to some flooding. In contrast, house fires occur all over the country in a much more evenhanded distribution.

The *social* distribution of natural hazard impacts, however, is not as well known. To the extent that different kinds of households are attracted to different areas of the country, the geographical distribution of disasters affects some parts of the population more than others. The types of structures inhabited by, say, the poor as opposed to the affluent may make some families more susceptible to the impacts of natural hazards. And so on through a list of the ways in which households differ one from the other.

It cannot be expected that that social characteristics of households will account for much of the variation in natural hazard impacts. Hazards affect households so infrequently that even if some are more likely to be seriously affected by, say, floods, the vast majority of such types of households will live unscathed through any given period. In addition, widespread hazard events, such as hurricanes or earthquakes, affect large areas that are inhabited by a wide variety of households and can hardly be expected to single out particular types of households for especially hard treatment.

Table 4.11 contains victimization hazard rates by selected household characteristics. The entries in the table are the num-

TABLE 4.11
Hazard Victimizations (1970–1980) per 1,000 Households by Selected Household Characteristics

Household characteristics	Fires	Floods	Hurricanes	Tornadoes	Earthquakes	Combined hazards	N
A. Age of head of household							
Under 30	41.7	22.1	19.6	78.1	12.8	174.3	(2,037)
30–44	46.3	23.3	29.4	72.0	11.5	182.4	(4,085)
45–64	35.9	17.2	24.7	64.2	10.8	152.8	(4,175)
65 and over	15.9	12.9	17.9	32.3	4.0	82.9	(2,014)
B. Tenure							
Renter	42.1	22.0	18.5	55.9	12.2	150.8	(3,184)
Owner	35.2	17.5	25.5	65.4	9.8	152.4	(9,421)
C. Place of residence							
Rural	36.3	22.1	22.8	77.1	4.1	162.4	(2,673)
Small city	32.8	19.7	17.6	65.1	8.1	143.2	(3,351)
Suburb	38.9	14.7	31.2	56.8	14.7	156.3	(2,853)
Medium-sized city	33.2	19.5	30.2	66.3	8.3	157.6	(2,050)
Large city	49.8	20.2	17.0	49.2	20.8	157.1	(1,585)
D. Number of persons in household							
1 Person	26.6	19.1	20.6	43.6	7.8	111.8	(2,039)
2 Persons	30.3	17.8	18.9	50.7	9.8	127.5	(3,867)
3–5 Persons	43.3	18.5	26.5	77.2	10.9	176.4	(5,777)
6 or more	62.8	26.7	34.9	65.1	10.5	200.0	(860)

E. Household race						
White	35.5	19.1	23.0	67.1	9.6	154.2	(11,284)
Black	52.8	15.5	31.3	29.0	10.4	138.7	(966)
Other nonwhite	39.6	18.5	26.4	34.3	26.4	145.1	(379)
F. Sex of respondent						
Female	37.5	17.1	21.6	54.6	10.0	141.3	(7,997)
Male	34.9	20.6	25.6	73.7	10.6	165.3	(5,008)
G. Region						
Pacific	35.8	10.7	6.6	26.3	84.7	163.5	(838)
Mountain	42.0	14.8	4.9	42.0	17.3	121.0	(405)
East North Central	37.9	13.8	10.6	98.8	8.1	169.2	(2,825)
West North Central	31.1	21.0	8.4	89.2	4.2	154.0	(1,188)
West South Central	48.2	19.8	34.8	78.3	3.2	184.1	(1,265)
East South Central	30.8	19.1	62.6	41.7	7.4	184.7	(942)
South Atlantic	40.3	13.4	36.5	42.4	2.5	135.1	(2,384)
Middle Atlantic	30.8	31.7	22.2	41.2	4.3	130.1	(2,113)
New England	32.0	18.4	18.4	31.0	1.0	100.8	(1,032)
H. Household income						
Under $9,000	35.6	20.8	21.7	53.7	8.8	140.7	(3,312)
$9,000–$15,000	45.3	22.0	17.5	57.6	11.6	153.9	(1,546)
$15,000–$20,000	42.0	20.4	28.4	72.6	9.1	172.5	(1,762)
$20,000–$25,000	36.6	16.6	25.8	79.1	9.6	167.7	(2,403)
$25,000–$35,000	27.3	23.9	34.1	64.8	6.8	157.0	(293)
$35,000 and over	41.4	20.7	33.1	91.0	17.1	203.3	(1,692)

bers of households per 1,000 households that experienced a victimization instance of the relevant hazard during the period 1970–1980. Thus, the first entry in the upper-left-hand corner of the table states that out of every 1,000 households whose heads were 30 or under, 41.7 experienced nontrivial household fires during the 1970–1980 period.[11]

Section A of Table 4.11 indicates how victimizations of households varied with the age of the head. By and large, households headed by younger persons were more likely to be victimized. Thus, 41.7 per 1,000 of the households headed by someone under 30 had a serious household fire. The rates increased slightly to 46.3 for households with heads between 30 and 44 and then declined to 35.9 and 15.9 for households in the two oldest age groups. Similar patterns are shown for floods and hurricanes. For these three hazards, households whose heads were between 30 and 44 had the highest rates, and the oldest households (with heads over 65) had the lowest rates. In contrast, tornadoes and earthquakes had a more regular pattern, with the youngest households having the highest rates and the oldest the smallest. The most consistent finding in Table 4.11 across all natural hazard types is the much lower incidence of victimization for the oldest households. As the rates per 1,000 households for all hazards combined show (last column on the right), the oldest households (heads over 65) had rates that were about half those of the younger group.

In part, these age differences reflect the correlates of age that affect exposure to natural hazard events. Older households are more likely to be home owners and thus to live in better structures.

Section B considers tenure differentials in hazard victimization. Overall, there was not much difference between households that rented and those that owned. However, renters were slightly

[11]While annualized rates might have appeared to be appropriate, the telescoping effect of recall would have overestimated the rates for younger households and produced inflated rates for such households and for any age-related household characteristics.

more likely to have experienced nontrivial fires, floods, and earthquakes, whereas owners were more likely to have been victimized by hurricanes and tornadoes. These patterns, we suspect, reflect the structural and locational differences among rental and owner-occupied units in the typical housing stocks of American communities.

Section C tabulates rates by place of residence. No clear dominant pattern appears consistently across the five hazard types. Large city residence was most likely to expose a household to a higher risk from household fires and earthquakes, and small-city residence was likely to lower all risks. However, no other pattern emerges, and even these patterns are not very pronounced.

Section D considers the influence of household size on hazard victimization. Clearly, larger households are more likely to have had nontrivial fires, the incidence per 1,000 households rising from 26.6 for one-person households to 62.8 for those composed of six or more. Although larger households generally appear to have been exposed to more risk, the patterns with respect to other hazards are not as clear-cut as in the case of household fires. Of course, household size is related in a complicated way to age—with both younger persons and the very old more likely to live in small households—and hence some of these patterns may simply reflect that fact alone.

Racial differences among households are considerable in Section E. No consistent pattern of racial differences is shown. Black households were more likely to experience nontrivial household fires and hurricanes, but whites were more likely to be victims of nontrivial floods and tornadoes. Other nonwhites (mainly Hispanic) were much more likely than either to experience earthquake victimization. These ethnic patterns very likely reflect housing conditions and regional concentrations.

Sex differences (based on the sex of the respondent) are also unclear. Indeed, because males and females in a majority of the households were reporting for the entire household, there should not have been very much in the way of such differences. Of course, in single-person and single-adult households, only one adult was available, and hence such respondents represented largely their own personal experiences. Such sex differences would very likely disappear if we held other information about the households constant. In any event, considered by itself, the sex of the respondents had its strongest effect on tornado victimization, with male respondents being considerably more likely to report serious tornado events than females.

Section G tabulates nontrivial experience rates by each of the nine major census regions of the United States. Regional differences appear with respect to all of the natural hazards considered. Victimizations by fire appear to have been more frequent in the Mountain and West South Central states and least frequent in New England and the Middle Atlantic states. Nontrivial floods show a rather flat regional profile: the Pacific and South Atlantic states had the fewest flood victimizations, and the highest rates were to be found in the Middle Atlantic[12] and the West North Central states.

As is to be expected, hurricane victimizations clustered heavily in the Gulf and South Atlantic states, with only a few victims to be found in the Pacific or Mountain states.[13]

The regional clustering of tornado victimization is also quite pronounced, with high rates in the East and West North Central and the West South Central states, the states through which Tornado Alley passes.

Finally, earthquakes show a pattern of very high incidence in the Pacific states, as expected, with low rates almost everywhere else. Indeed, earthquakes show the strongest regional patterning, the victimization rates per 1,000 households being 84.7 for the Pacific states and 1.0 for New England.[14]

[12]Undoubtedly reflecting the widespread effects of the flooding accompanying hurricane Agnes in 1972.

[13]Possibly reflecting the experiences of households that had migrated from the South Atlantic and Gulf states during the period 1970–1980.

[14]Note that these rates counted each household at its present location, not necessarily at the residence in which the household was residing at the time the hazard experience took place. Hence, it may well be the case that all the New England households claiming an earthquake experience actually were living in

Section H considers total household income (as reported). No particular pattern shows up with respect to this measure of household socioeconomic status. The least affluent households tended to report fewer serious hazard events, possibly reflecting the lower incomes of the aged. The most affluent households reported more tornado and earthquake victimizations, but no other particular patterns appear.

The findings of Table 4.11 consider only one household characteristic at a time. To the extent that such characteristics are interrelated, any of the findings might reflect some of the others. In short, the effects of age shown in that table might simply reflect the fact that the age distributions of regional populations may vary. In order to estimate the separate or "net" effects of each of the household characteristics, we have calculated regressions, as shown in Table 4.12.

The dependent variables in the regression equations of Table 4.12 are the number of hazard victimizations from 1970 to 1980 of the types in question per 1,000 households. Each row of the table presents regression coefficients (unstandardized), with the standard errors of the coefficients in parentheses below. The interpretation of the coefficients is fairly straightforward: The coefficient −.6652 for age in the column labeled "Fires" means that for each year of age, holding everything else in the equation constant, fire victims per 1,000 households occurring during the period 1970–1980 dropped by .6652. That is, 1,000 households whose heads were 25 years of age reported 29.9 more household fires than 1,000 households whose heads were 70 years of age. Similarly, 1,000 households that owned their dwellings reported 6.6 fewer household fires for that period than households that rented.

Note that we have included in the equations a variable that

---

the San Fernando Valley in 1971 and hence were reporting a California rather than a New England event. Given the migration and mobility patterns of the United States population over an 11-year period, considerable portions of the households studied may have lived in several regions in that period. (Annual interstate migration rates range between 3% and 4%, cumulating to about 25% over a decade.)

TABLE 4.12

Regressions of Hazard Victimizations on Selected Household Characteristics (N = 10,701) (Dependent Variables are Numbers of Hazard Victimizations during 1970–1980 per 1,000 Households)

Independent variables	Fires	Floods	Hurricanes	Tornadoes	Earthquakes	Combined hazards
Household characteristics						
Age of head						
b =	−.6652***	−.2582***	.0633	−.8391***	−.1231	−1.946***
SE =	(.144)	(.104)	(.116)	(.184)	(.076)	(.305)
Years in existence[a]						
b =	1.870**	.3772	.4448	2.029*	.3079	5.022***
SE =	(.713)	(.512)	(.572)	(.910)	(.376)	(1.51)
Number of persons						
b =	4.39***	.5248	2.066*	2.513	.2773	9.761***
SE =	(1.23)	(.884)	(.988)	(1.57)	(.649)	(2.60)
Household income						
b =	−.1754	−.0564	.2444	.7555**	.0058	.7808*
SE =	(.176)	(.126)	(.141)	(.224)	(.009)	(.372)
Owner						
b =	−6.656	−3.468	2.370	−3.423	−.1411	−11.35
SE =	(4.78)	(3.43)	(3.83)	(6.10)	(2.52)	(10.1)
White						
b =	−1.630	6.639	1.209	34.18***	1.910	38.41**
SE =	(6.20)	(4.46)	(4.98)	(7.92)	(3.27)	(13.1)
Other nonwhite[b]						
b =	−5.372	4.094	7.243	8.409	.6812	15.01
SE =	(12.2)	(8.73)	(9.76)	(15.5)	(6.41)	(25.7)

Male respondent						
b =	-3.798	2.102	2.013	13.38**	-.6549	15.04
SE =	(3.78)	(2.72)	(3.04)	(4.83)	(2.00)	(8.01)
Place of residence[c]						
Small city						
b =	-2.205	-2.160	-3.256	-8.154	3.825	-12.0
SE =	(5.27)	(3.79)	(4.23)	(6.72)	(2.78)	(11.1)
Medium-sized city						
b =	-3.621	-1.468	10.36*	6.453	-.3198	-1.659
SE =	(6.06)	(4.35)	(4.86)	(7.73)	(3.19)	(12.8)
Suburbs						
b =	2.691	-7.260	9.652*	-19.93**	7.386	-7.660
SE =	(5.55)	(3.99)	(4.45)	(7.08)	(2.93)	(11.7)
Large city						
b =	12.22	-1.704	-1.220	18.89*	10.00**	.1310
SE =	(6.71)	(4.82)	(5.38)	(8.56)	(3.54)	(.142)
Region[d]						
Pacific						
b =	-7.338	-3.475	-9.266	-14.69	66.60***	40.20
SE =	(12.5)	(8.99)	(10.0)	(16.0)	(6.59)	(26.5)
West North Central						
b =	-10.10	6.071	4.862	45.45**	12.06*	34.15
SE =	(11.9)	(8.55)	(9.56)	(15.2)	(6.28)	(25.2)
West South Central						
b =	4.990	5.476	30.18**	38.40*	-14.15	64.83**
SE =	(11.8)	(8.48)	(9.47)	(15.1)	(6.22)	(25.0)
East North Central						
b =	5.319	.5721	5.509	56.67***	-9.057	47.16*
SE =	(10.9)	(7.89)	(8.82)	(14.0)	(5.80)	(23.2)

(continued)

TABLE 4.12 (Continued)

Independent variables	Fires	Floods	Hurricanes	Tornadoes	Earthquakes	Combined hazards
East South Central						
$b =$	−11.42	4.862	58.93***	24.13	−8.958	67.43**
$SE =$	(12.3)	(8.86)	(9.90)	(15.7)	(6.50)	(26.1)
New England						
$b =$	−10.27	3.957	12.87	−13.19	−15.81**	−22.49
$SE =$	(12.2)	(8.73)	(9.75)	(15.5)	(6.41)	(25.1)
Middle Atlantic						
$b =$	−13.24	17.73*	17.81*	1.837	−13.51*	10.60
$SE =$	(11.2)	(8.07)	(9.01)	(14.3)	(5.92)	(23.8)
South Atlantic						
$b =$	−2.142	−26.87***	31.94***	3.74	−14.49	18.71
$SE =$	(11.2)	(8.01)	(8.95)	(14.2)	(5.88)	(23.6)
Intercept						
$b =$	53.81***	20.45*	−14.28	17.03	17.09	94.13**
$SE =$	(14.9)	(10.7)	(12.0)	(19.1)	(7.88)	(31.6)
R^2	.007**	.004**	.014**	.022**	.041**	.015**

[a]Number of years (1–11) household was in existence during period 1970–1980.
[b]Dummy variables: Omitted category is "black."
[c]Dummy variables: Omitted category is "rural."
[d]Dummy variables: Omitted category is Mountain States.

$*p < .05$
$**p < .01$
$***p < .001$

measures the time a household had been in existence during the period 1970–1980. This variable holds constant the variations in exposure to risk occasioned by the fact that some households (about one in three) were formed during the period 1970–1980 and hence were not exposed to risk during the entire 11-year period.

At the bottom of each of the columns in Table 4.12 are the R^2's for the equations. This coefficient is a measure of the extent to which variations in the exposure to risk are "accounted for" by the variables in the equations. Because the overwhelming majority of all households did not have any nontrivial natural-hazard experiences during the period under study but nevertheless differed among themselves in age, tenure, and so on, these independent variables cannot make much of a difference in determining exposure to risk. Hence, none of the equations are expected to "account for" much of the difference in hazard victimization. Indeed, such is the case. Less than 1% of the variation in fire and flood victimizations can be accounted for, and the other equations also explain very modest amounts. Indeed, we can do best in accounting for earthquake victimizations ($R^2 = .041$), but by any standards usually applied to social research, this is also a very modest amount.

The regression equation pertaining to fire victimizations is shown in the left-hand column of Table 4.12. The major influences on nontrivial fire experiences were age, years in existence, and number of persons in the household. Fire victimizations declined with increasing age, increased with years in existence, and increased with the number of persons in the household. None of the other factors in the equations is significant. Note that some of the differences we saw in Table 4.11 have now declined in significance: Renters appear no more likely than owners to be victims of fire, once we take into account the fact that renters tend to be younger than owners and to be recently formed households.

Despite the low R^2 for the fire equation, the differences in incidence among extreme types of households can be quite large. Thus, a household that has been in existence throughout the period and is headed by a person who is 30 years old has a predicted victimization rate (per 1,000 households) of 54.4, as compared with 9.1 for a household with a 70-year-old head that was formed in 1980.

The equation for flood victimizations is somewhat weaker than for fires, with only 0.4% of the variance being explained. Only the age of the household head makes any difference, along with living in a Middle Atlantic state. All the other elements in the equation yield insignificant coefficients. Thus, households headed by a 30-year-old person and living in the Middle Atlantic states had a victimization rate (per 1,000 households) of 30.43, as compared with 2.38 for households headed by 70-year-olds living in the Mountain states.

Exposure to hurricane victimization is somewhat better predicted: $R^2 = .014$. A different set of predictors play the important roles in hurricanes. As might be expected, regional location constituted a strong influence, with residence in the West South Central and Middle Atlantic states being important, along with living in medium-sized cities or suburbs. Among household characteristics, only the size of the household made a difference, with larger households more likely to be victims of a hurricane. Again, the extremes can be quite dramatic: A six-person household living in a medium-sized city in the South Atlantic region had an expected victimization rate of 38.7 (per 1,000 households), as compared with essentially zero for a comparably sized household that lived in the Mountain states.

Tornadoes are even better predicted than hurricanes, with R^2 for the equation reaching .022. Regional differences are strong, with the Central state regions having significantly high positive coefficients. But household characteristics also made a difference: Older persons were less likely to have suffered a serious tornado or windstorm experience. Whites were more likely than blacks, perhaps reflecting the fact that blacks are mainly to be found in the larger cities within those regions. A significant positive coefficient was also found for years of household existence, indicating that tornadoes occurred at about the same rate each year and that the longer a household had been in existence, the more likely it was to have a serious tornado experience. Perhaps most intriguing of all is the high positive coefficient for male respondents, a finding for which there appears to be little interpretation.[15] More sensible is the positive coefficient for income, indicating that upper-income households were more likely to be victims of a tornado or windstorm of more than minimal intensity.

The range of experience caught by the tornado equation is also best illustrated by taking an extreme case: A white household headed by a 30-year-old, reported through a male respondent, with an annual income of $40,000 and living in a large city in the East North Central region, had an estimated rate of 139.12 tornado victimizations per 1,000 households. In contrast, a black family living in the Mountain states, headed by a 30-year-old person, earning $40,000 per year and living in a rural area, had an expected rate of tornado victimization of essentially zero per 1,000 for the period 1970–1980.

Earthquake victimizations appear to be primarily a locational matter. Persons living in large cities were more likely to claim nontrivial earthquake experiences, but no other characteristics of households, such as income, race, age, or years in existence, played any role. The main determinants appear to be regional, with a very high positive coefficient for living in the Pacific states and with low negative ones for living in New England and the Middle Atlantic states.

The extreme predictions are as follows: A Los Angeles family would face an experience rate of 93.96 (per 1,000), whereas a New England rural family would face a rate of only 1.28 (per 1,000).

Considering the five combined hazards experiences (as in the last column of Table 4.12), we note that it is most hazardous to belong to a young, affluent, and large white household that lives in the hurricane or tornado belts. As in the case of the single

---

[15]One might speculate that the probability of a male's answering the telephone interview was differentially distributed among areas, but that explanation is unconvincing.

hazards considered separately, the equations do not predict very well the kinds of households that will have these experiences— the R^2 for the combined hazards equation being only .015. In short, some households are exposed to a greater risk, but the overall level of risk is not high enough for us to be able to predict with any accuracy which kinds families will be disproportionately affected.

COMPARISON WITH OTHER NOXIOUS EVENTS

It is useful to compare the social distribution of hazard experiences, as shown in Table 4.12, with the social distribution of the "other noxious events" discussed in an earlier section, as in Table 4.13. In that table, we have combined the noxious events into the three categories discussed earlier: "Other Natural Hazards" (consisting of experiences with the 5 natural hazard events of the 17), "Bad-Luck Events" (experiences such as auto accidents and unemployment), and "Personal Breakdown Events" (such as depression and bankruptcy). Each of the three types of events, plus a combined index encompassing all three, is used as a dependent variable in regression equations having the identical structure to those shown in Table 4.12.

Although the sizes of the coefficients in Table 4.13 cannot be compared with those of Table 4.12, it is valid to compare which household characteristics are statistically significant. Thus, Table 4.13 indicates that the age of the head of the house was consistently important for experiences with noxious events, older households being less likely to have had such experiences during the period 1970–1980. For the five natural hazards, the age of the head of the house was significant for some and not for others. Younger households were simply more likely to be exposed to risk, especially bad-luck events and personal breakdowns.

More recently established households (less than 11 years in existence) were no more likely to be exposed to a risk of having

TABLE 4.13

Regression of Noxious Events on Selected Household Characteristics (N = 1,035) (Dependent Variables are Number of Events per 1,000 Households during 1970–1980)

Independent variables	Other natural hazards	Bad-luck events	Personal breakdown events	Combined noxious events
Household characteristics				
Age of head of house				
b =	-3.871*	-4.060**	-2.718**	-10.87***
SE =	(1.52)	(1.65)	(1.04)	(2.86)
Years in existence[a]				
b =	5.495	-8.130	-9.183	-12.08
SE =	(7.87)	(8.51)	(5.24)	(14.8)
Number of persons				
b =	.6419	4.934	-1.015	4.493
SE =	(6.91)	(7.48)	(4.60)	(12.9)
Owner				
b =	-23.55	-16.70	-98.24**	-140.1
SE =	(53.9)	(58.3)	(35.8)	(101.2)
White				
b =	250.1**	159.1*	58.29	467.2**
SE =	(74.4)	(80.5)	(49.5)	(139.7)
Other non-white[b]				
b =	-22.49	192.9	-36.56	133.2
SE =	(14.1)	(152.1)	(93.5)	(263.9)

(continued)

Table 4.13 (Continued)

Independent variables	Other natural hazards	Bad-luck events	Personal breakdown events	Combined noxious events
Household income (000's)				
b =	3.887	.8928	-1.313	3.442
SE =	(2.11)	(2.28)	(1.403)	(3.97)
Male respondent				
b =	-.7098	-84.53	-1.520	-87.83
SE =	(44.9)	(48.6)	(2.99)	(84.4)
Place of residence[c]				
Small city				
b =	-6.116	35.59	-24.14	5.220
SE =	(60.7)	(65.6)	(40.4)	(113.9)
Medium-sized city				
b =	-22.16	60.06	9.610	46.31
SE =	(70.8)	(76.6)	(4.71)	(132.9)
Suburbs				
b =	29.77	53.15	-29.39	52.98
SE =	(62.8)	(67.9)	(41.7)	(117.8)
Large city				
b =	121.3	240.35**	54.70	414.4**
SE =	(76.4)	(82.6)	(50.8)	(143.4)
Region[d]				
Pacific				
b =	-442.2**	83.85	28.54	330.3
SE =	(149.3)	(161.5)	(99.3)	(280.4)

West North Central				
b =	396.4**	103.6	1.015	293.2
SE =	(140.2)	(151.6)	(93.2)	(263.2)
West South Central				
b =	−187.5	20.75	114.5	52.98
SE =	(140.)	(15.1)	(93.1)	(262.9)
East North Central				
b =	206.6	22.6	65.69	294.4
SE =	(129.6)	(14.0)	(86.2)	(24.4)
East South Central				
b =	−240.4	−80.58	25.33	−295.7
SE =	(142.0)	(153.7)	(94.5)	(266.8)
New England				
b =	132.0	67.71	15.85	215.1
SE =	(142.5)	(154.2)	(94.8)	(267.6)
Middle Atlantic				
b =	10.76	51.80	−16.58	23.89
SE =	(131.2)	(141.9)	(87.3)	(246.4)
South Atlantic				
b =	200.2	5.330	29.64	−165.2
SE =	(130.7)	(141.4)	(86.9)	(245.3)
Intercept				
b =	433.6**	533.7***	398.0***	1381.4***
SE =	(170.1)	(184.1)	(113.7)	(319.5)
R^2	.135	.037	.051	.084

[a]Number of years (1–11) household was in existence during period 1970–1980.
[b]Dummy variables: Omitted category is "black."
[c]Dummy variables: Omitted category is "rural."
[d]Dummy variables: Omitted category is Mountain states.

*$p < .05$
**$p < .01$
***$p < .001$

such noxious experiences. Similarly negative findings also characterize household size and income.

Owners were somewhat less exposed than renters to personal breakdown events. And white households were more likely to experience the natural hazards, most likely snowstorms and hailstorms, that were so large a component of these additional hazards. Whites were also more likely to experience "bad-luck" events, and these were also more likely to occur for those who lived in large cities.

Finally, the regional variables appear to show that the Pacific states are less likely to experience these natural hazards and the West North Central states are more likely to experience them. Again, this pattern probably reflects the fact that snowstorms and hailstorms dominate this index in terms of frequency. It is therefore hardly surprising that snowstorm and hailstorm experiences were reported infrequently in California and frequently in the western portions of the Northern Great Plains.

The patterns of correlates for the 17 noxious events are different from those discussed in the last section. Hence, at least one explanation is ruled out: that the respondents were simply complaining about their lives and elevating minor happenings into major traumas, as would be suggested if all the events had the same distribution among households. On the contrary, it appears that noxious events and natural hazards behave differently, the former being heavily dependent on region and the latter being more dependent on household characteristics.

SUMMARY

Experience with natural hazards—fires, floods, tornadoes, hurricanes, and earthquakes—is relatively frequent for the American population as a whole. Over the decade of the 1970s, about one household in four experienced such an event. Roughly half these experiences were "trivial" in the sense that no injuries or property damages were incurred. Thus, the rate at which families are actually victimized by natural hazards is on the order of 10%–15% per decade.

Vulnerability to hazard victimization appears to be conditioned mainly by geography, and much less so by the social and demographic characteristics of households. Net of the well-known regional differences, victimization by natural hazard is more-or-less randomly distributed over the population.

Of course, knowing that a household experienced a hazard event, or even was victimized by one, says little about the magnitude of loss. Some victims suffer minor amounts of damage, and other substantially larger amounts. The nature and magnitude of losses sustained by hazard victims are the topics of the next chapter.

CHAPTER 5

Deaths, Injuries, Damages, and Total Costs

INTRODUCTION

The total costs to a household of a natural hazard event consist of all the burdens incurred because of the event minus any benefits that may have accrued. When we recognize that the burdens can cover a miscellaneous congeries of troubles, only some of which can be translated into monetary terms, then the task of estimating costs becomes formidable. Benefits present no less a problem for measurement. Indeed, because the benefits from a disaster are likely to be indirect or to occur as side effects, they may be difficult to detect at all.

Nonetheless, some costs can be approximated fairly accurately, especially when they are easily converted into monetary terms. The damages to property and possessions and the direct monetary costs of injuries can be estimated through reports from victimized households. Because the dollar values of damages are usually ascertained necessarily when repairs are made or when insurance claims are filed, we can expect that many—if not most—households know at least the approximate sums involved. Similarly, the dollar costs of medical care are known from bills paid or from medical insurance claims made.

These, to be sure, are not the only costs borne by a household experiencing a natural hazard. The trauma inflicted by the experience itself, the impairment of functioning, and the disruption of normal routines are perhaps less tangible, but equally real. In addition, households may experience indirect effects of the event involving the disruption of public services, of normal economic activity in the local community, and so on. The monetary costs discussed in this chapter do not include any of these costs. Here, rather, we deal with the consequences of hazards that result directly in damages and injuries. Furthermore, only those costs that have been recorded in monetary terms in the memories (or records) of our respondents are counted. The restriction to relatively straightforward damages and injuries, of course, is not a judgment on the importance of these other—less palpable—costs, but a confession of the limits of the research methods employed in this project.

A cautionary note: The period 1970 through 1980 was also a period in which inflationary processes drastically changed the purchasing power of our currency. The reader is advised to keep this fact in mind when reading dollar amounts that have not been converted into constant dollars. Of course, where especially appropriate, such calculations have been made, as noted in the legends of statistical tables and in the text.

The issues addressed here are primarily descriptive ones: What was the distribution of costs? From what sorts of damages and injuries did they arise? What kinds of households were likely to suffer large rather than small amounts of monetary costs? And so on. The focus in all cases is on what might be called the "gross costs" incurred as a result of the disaster—that is, the initial damage done and injury inflicted as a direct result of the event. The "net cost," that portion of the original cost that remained after insurance claims has been paid, relief monies provided, and other forms of assistance rendered, is considered in some detail in the following chapter.

The findings reported in this chapter are derived from the mail follow-up survey whose implementation was discussed in Chapter 3. With due allowances for nonresponse, the mail survey sample can be taken as a probability sample of surviving house-

TABLE 5.1
Frequency of Hazard Types in Mail Survey

Type of hazard	Numer of cases	Percentage
Fires	268	16.5
Floods	152	9.4
Hurricanes	261	16.1
Tornadoes	581	35.8
Earthquakes	363	22.3
Total	1,625	100.0

holds that experienced one or more of the five hazard events during the 11 years 1970–1980.[1] Owing both to refusals to cooperate in the study after screening (which, it will be recalled, was correlated with the extent of damages inflicted by the event) and to the decision to "sample out" a fraction of the "trivial" hurricane, tornado, and earthquake events that were identified in the screening interviews, the final sample of victims was probably skewed somewhat in favor of victims suffering higher-than-average costs. As noted previously, the final sample was a sample of both households and hazard events. The number of households involved was just under 1,300, but these households supplied victimization data for a total of 1,625 events. This latter number constituted the case base for all analyses reported in this and the following chapter. Table 5.1 shows the distribution of these 1,625 events according to the type of hazard each represents.

ESTIMATING "TOTAL DOLLAR COSTS"

Total dollar costs can be defined as the dollar value of damages to property and possessions, plus the dollar value of medical care resulting from hazard-related injuries, plus all other

[1]Because the study is retrospective, the sampling strategies employed did not cover households in which all family members died as a result of the event, or households that emigrated to other countries subsequent to their victimization, or households that were dissolved for any other reason.

expenses related to the event. Total dollar cost is a critical variable in this chapter, and hence, a detailed description of how it was constructed is important.

We adopted a strategy of asking questions about specific kinds of damages and the dollar amounts involved, followed by a summary question that asked for an overall estimate of the sum of those damages (and any other monetary costs borne). The entire series of questions was prefaced by the following filter questions:

> Was anyone in your family or household injured or killed, or did anyone become physically sick as a result of the event?
>
> Did you and your family or household suffer any damage to your house or apartment or damage to your furniture and personal property as a result of the event?

Any respondent who indicated that someone had been injured or killed was then asked a series of questions on the costs of the medical care involved (if any). Similarly, anyone who indicated any property damage was asked a series of questions on damages to specific categories of property or possessions (e.g., roof, walls, jewelry, and cars), as well as follow-up questions on the dollar amounts involved.

A summary question that followed these two series was then asked:

> What were the total dollar costs to you and your family that resulted from the event? Please include the costs that resulted from the injuries and damages that you listed in Questions 12 and 14, any losses of valuables in Question 16, costs of living in other places in Question 18, and any other expenses you had as a result of the event.

(See Appendix B for details on this series of questions.) Note, then, that two estimates of "total cost" are available.[2] The first is the respondent's own estimate of total dollar losses, and the second is the sum of responses given to each of the category-by-

---

[2]To emphasize, throughout this chapter, we use the term cost to refer to the monetary loss involved, regardless of whether the amount was reimbursed through insurance or any other financial aid.

category cost questions. Rather than making an *a priori* decision about which of these was the more valid measure, we simply compared the two estimates and took whichever was the higher as the household's actual total cost figure.

There is, of course, yet a third estimate available: that provided by respondents in the course of the screening interview. Although the screening estimates were made "on the spot" and preceded the more detailed estimates made in the mail follow-up by weeks or even months, the "total dollar cost" variable employed in this chapter correlates at about .70 with the estimates obtained in the screening interview.[3] This correlation gives one some confidence in the reliability of the cost data available for this analysis.

Defining Serious Hazard Events

As discussed in Chapter 4, to "experience" a hazard event does not necessarily imply that people were injured or property losses incurred. Hence, as in that chapter, we are concerned to separate "serious" from "minor" events. Because the cost information contained in the mail survey was much more detailed, we can be more certain about the resulting classification here than we were in Chapter 4.

For purposes of the present chapter, a "serious" event was any reported victimization that caused nonzero total dollar costs (whatever the actual dollar value of the loss), or that injured (or killed) at least one member of the household, or, of course, both. This, to be sure, is a lenient definition of *serious*. A home fire that destroyed a five-dollar wastepaper basket would, for example, qualify as "serious" by our definition, as would one that destroyed the whole house.

By this (admittedly lenient) standard, most of the events re-

[3]The correlation was computed by converting the dollar sums involved into logs so that the correlation would not be too affected by the small number of very large damage estimates.

maining in the sample at this point qualified as serious (see Table 5.2); earthquake events provide the main exception. The table shows the proportion of events that caused any damages or any injuries. To emphasize, the table shows *events*, not households, and so the case bases are as shown in Table 5.1 (less those with missing data on appropriate variables).

The results of Table 5.2 are fairly straightforward and require no extended discussion. Most of the fire events reported by our respondents (86%) resulted in at least some dollar damages; the same is true, in lesser degrees, of floods (76%), tornadoes (65%), and hurricanes (55%). Most earthquake events, in contrast, inflicted no dollar damages; only 14% of the reported events caused any dollar damage at all. These differences are generally as one would expect, given the nature of the events themselves: The more intense and localized hazard types (e.g., fires) show higher proportions inflicting damages, whereas the more diffuse types (e.g., hurricanes, earthquakes, and tremors) show lower proportions.

Property damage was by far more common a consequence of a hazard than personal injury or death. The proportions of reported events causing personal injuries varied from 9% (fires) down to

TABLE 5.2
Percentage of Events Causing Any Damage[a] and Injury by Type of Hazard

Serious event	Fires	Floods	Hurricanes	Tornadoes	Earthquakes
Percentage of events with damages[a]	85.7	76.4	55.2	64.8	14.4
Percentage of events resulting in any injury	9.3	7.6	2.4	1.8	2.3
Percentage of events resulting in death	0.4	0.7	0.0	0.3	0.0
All other injury	5.2	1.3	0.8	0.8	0.6
Physical illness	3.0	4.6	1.5	0.3	1.4
N =	(267)	(151)	(261)	(581)	(363)

[a]Defined as damages valued by respondents as nonzero dollars.

about 2% (tornadoes); and death was even less common, being reported in fewer than 1% of all cases, irrespective of hazard type.

INJURIES AND THEIR MONETARY COSTS

Although injury was not a common consequence of a hazard event, as we have just seen, some injuries did nevertheless occur, and when they occurred, the impact on the household could be quite traumatic (and expensive). In the extreme case, the death of a family member, the ensuing costs would include some incalculable grief plus the costs of funeral services, burial, and so on. A serious, even if nonfatal, injury would normally have associated hospitalization or medical care costs, costs resulting from lost wages, etc. For these more-or-less obvious reasons, the true costs of injuries incurred in natural hazard events are certainly more important than would be indicated by the relatively low percentages reported in Table 5.2. In the present section, then, we explore more fully the costs associated with personal injury.

Table 5.3 reproduces the percentages of reported events that were accompanied by any injury whatever. As noted previously, the hazards most likely to result in injuries were fires and floods (9.3% and 7.6%, respectively) and to a much lesser extent hurricanes, tornadoes, and earthquakes (occurring in approximately 2% of all such events). As can be seen from the table, not all injuries were equally serious or harmful. (Stated more precisely, not all hazard events caused equally serious personal injuries.) In some cases, for example, the injuries involved were not accompanied by any medical expenses whatsoever: The proportions range from about 12% of all fire injuries up to about half the injuries resulting from earthquakes. There is also wide variability in the percentages of injurious events causing injuries sufficiently serious to require a doctor's care or hospitalization. Households sustaining an injury due to a fire required a doctor's care 45.8% of the time and hospitalization in 33% of the cases. By far, fire-related injuries were the most serious, with almost 80% of the

TABLE 5.3

Selected Characteristics of Injury, Households with Any Injury, Medical Costs,[a] and Insurance Reimbursement by Type of Hazard

	Fire	Flood	Hurricane	Tornado	Earthquake
N of events	(268)	(152)	(261)	(581)	(363)
Percentage with any injury	9.3	7.6	2.4	1.8	2.3
Only events with injuries					
Percentage with no medical costs	12.5	18.2	16.7	40.0	50.0
Percentage requiring doctor's care	45.8	27.3	50.0	30.0	12.5
Percentage requiring hospitalization	33.3	27.3	0.0	30.0	0.0
Average cost[a] of medical care	$300	$41	$105	$48	—[b]
Median cost[a] of medical care	$ 99	$55	$ 98	$16	—[b]
N =	(16)	(5)	(5)	(6)	(0)
Injurious events with non-zero medical costs					
Percentage of households covered for injuries by insurance	67	33	20	83	25
N =	(21)	(9)	(5)	(6)	(4)

[a]Expressed in constant 1980 dollars.
[b]N too small.

households that sustained such injuries requiring formal medical care for their members. In contrast, injuries sustained in earthquakes and hurricanes never required hospitalization (over the extremely small number of injurious events available for this analysis). The percentages of events causing injuries sufficiently serious to warrant a doctor's attention varied between 12% and 50%. Given the numbers of cases available here, generalizations must of necessity be couched in terms of rough orders of magnitude: Over all hazard events contained in the final sample, roughly 1 in 20 resulted in personal injury (or death). Among only these injurious events, roughly 1 in 4 caused only very minor personal injuries, and the remainder were more serious, requiring hospitalization in the most extreme case, at the least a doctor's attention, or inflicting a nonzero medical cost on the victim.

Table 5.3 also reports the average costs of medical care associated with the injuries incurred in the hazard event(s). The averages reported are only for injury events causing nonzero medical costs. For the most part, the medical costs were not staggering. Fire-related injuries had the highest average medical care cost, $300, but half of the households had costs of $99 or less. The relatively high costs in fire events was very likely due to the nature of the injury, usually burns, which may have required more specialized care. The average medical costs of the remaining hazards were much lower, averaging only $41 for floods and $48 for tornadoes. By and large, the costs of medical care were not very high, and as the median dollar amounts indicate, they do not appear to have been serious threats to the finances of the households involved. As shown at the bottom of the table, the burden was further reduced through insurance coverage for all or part of the medical costs incurred, especially for fire- and tornado-related injuries.

In sum, relatively few hazard events involve personal injury, and among those that do, the dollar costs incurred as a result of the injury are relatively modest, especially once coverage by insurance is taken into account. As we see in a later section, the dollar costs incurred through property damage or destruction are substantially greater.

Households that reported any injury resulting from a hazard event were also asked to supply some information on the actual victims. For any given event, data were obtained on up to four victims. Age and sex at the time of the incident and a few additional descriptive items were obtained for each victim. Data on victim characteristics are shown in Table 5.4.

Overall, there was a slight tendency for females to be overrepresented among the injured. Across all hazard types, women comprised between 50% and 58% of all persons injured. The reasons are twofold: among adults, women outnumber men because of differences in longevity and hence should be overrepresented

TABLE 5.4
Selected Characteristics of Persons with Any Injury by Type of Hazard

Selected characteristics	Fires	Floods	Hurricanes	Tornadoes	Earthquakes
Sex of victim					
Males (percentage)	42.9	47.1	41.7	50.0	41.7
Age of victim					
Mean (years)	26	31	47	36	30
Median (years)	15	22	56	27	32
Percentage of victims unable to go to work or school because of injury	70.0	81.8	58.3	20.4	16.7
Percentage of victims still bothered by injury	24.2	35.7	11.1	20.0	16.7
Approximate N^a =	(35)	(18)	(12)	(12)	(12)

[a]Base fluctuates slightly from row to row because of missing data.

among the victims simply because there are more of them; moreover, women spend more time in the home than men and are thus exposed more to the risks of hazard events that strike the home.

There were also some differences with respect to the age of the victim, as shown in Section B. Fire victims tended to be fairly young: The average age was 26 years, and 50% of the victims were 15 years old or less. Flood and earthquake victims were also relatively young (about 30 years old on average). Tornado victims, in contrast, tended to be somewhat older (36 years on average), and hurricane victims tended to be older (47 years) than victims of all other hazards. In fact, half of the hurricane victims were 56 years or older. Several possible explanations for these age patterns could be advanced. The proclivity of children to play with matches, for example, may in part account for the low average age of the fire victims. Households at various stages in the life cycle may also make different kinds of decisions about where to locate their residences, and if, as seems possible, housing located in more hazardous areas (e.g., in the flood plains) tends to be less expensive, then younger families may self-select into relatively more hazardous housing. There is also very probably a regional effect present in these data: To illustrate, earthquakes tend to be experienced mainly in California, where the average age is lower than that for the nation as a whole; in like fashion, hurricanes are most commonly experienced along the southern coastal areas, where many retirement communities are located.

We also asked our respondents two direct questions regarding the seriousness of the injury sustained by the victim. First, had the person been unable to work or go to school for any period of time because of the injury? Second, did the injury still bother the person? By and large, the injuries reported by the respondents were, by these standards, serious ones. The large majority of fire and flood victims had been injured seriously enough to keep them from their normal work or school routines (70% and 82%, respectively). In addition, about one-quarter of fire victims and one-third of flood victims were still bothered by their injuries at the time of the survey. Though 58% of hurricane victims had been unable to attend work or school, only 11% sustained injuries that still bothered them at the time of the survey. Tornado and earthquake victims tended to be injured less severely: Most had been able to attend work or school, and relatively few still suffered from their injury.

INJURY RATES BY SELECTED HOUSEHOLD CHARACTERISTICS

Given that a household has experienced a disaster of one or another type, what factors influence whether an injury will also be sustained? In other words, are some kinds of households more "injury-prone" than others in a hazard event? Relevant data are shown in Table 5.5. For the purposes of this tabulation, a hazard event was considered injurious if anyone was killed, injured, or made physically ill as a result of the event, no matter how extensive or serious the injuries were. The cells in the table show "inju-

TABLE 5.5
Proportions Injured by Selected Household Characteristics

Selected characteristic	Proportions injured				
	Fire	Flood	Hurricane	Tornado	Earthquake
A. Age of oldest person at time of event					
Under 30	11.5%	11.1%	3.9%	3.0%	2.3%
N =	(104)	(72)	(77)	(200)	(131)
30–44	7.6%	0.0%	1.2%	1.1%	4.0%
N =	(79)	(30)	(80)	(182)	(100)
45–64	7.1%	6.2%	3.3%	0.0%	1.2%
N =	(56)	(32)	(61)	(128)	(87)
65 and over	11.8%	11.1%	0.0%	5.4%	0.0%
N =	(17)	(9)	(20)	(37)	(15)
B. Size of household at time of event					
1 person	7.7%	5.3%	0.0%	4.8%	3.8%
N =	(13)	(19)	(20)	(63)	(52)
2 persons	11.3%	2.9%	6.0%	1.6%	2.4%
N =	(53)	(34)	(67)	(121)	(84)
3–5 persons	8.7%	8.6%	1.5%	1.3%	1.2%
N =	(150)	(58)	(135)	(300)	(170)
6 or more	3.7%	0.0%	0.0%	0.0%	10.5%
N =	(27)	(14)	(14)	(32)	(19)
C. Tenure					
Rent	9.2%	4.9%	4.1%	1.1%	2.1%
N =	(65)	(41)	(49)	(92)	(95)
Own	8.1%	7.1%	2.0%	2.0%	2.5%
N =	(186)	(99)	(197)	(445)	(239)
D. Race					
White	9.0%	7.4%	2.0%	2.0%	2.0%
N =	(210)	(121)	(147)	(488)	(293)
Minority	5.9%	10.0%	2.6%	0.0%	5.4%
N =	(34)	(10)	(39)	(35)	(37)
E. Household income at time of event					
Under $10,000	15.0%	12.5%	5.0%	3.3%	3.3%
N =	(60)	(32)	(40)	(90)	(60)
$10,000–15,000	7.0%	11.4%	2.3%	1.0%	2.0%
N =	(57)	(35)	(43)	(102)	(49)
$15,000–20,000	12.0%	0.0%	0.0%	3.6%	2.1%
N =	(25)	(21)	(28)	(84)	(48)

TABLE 5.5   (*Continued*)

Selected characteristic	Proportions injured				
	Fire	Flood	Hurricane	Tornado	Earthquake
$20,000–25,000	4.8%	0.0%	0.0%	0.0%	2.5%
N =	(21)	(15)	(32)	(66)	(40)
$25,000–40,000	5.6%	0.0%	0.0%	1.2%	0.0%
N =	(36)	(7)	(42)	(80)	(64)
$40,000 and over	8.3%	0.0%	5.3%	2.6%	0.0%
N =	(12)	(6)	(19)	(39)	(26)
F. Context of disaster					
Isolated	8.6%	6.7%	7.8%	1.9%	1.0%
N =	(221)	(30)	(51)	(103)	(210)
Block	23.5%	0.0%	16.7%	0.0%	0.0%
N =	(17)	(8)	(6)	(18)	(4)
Neighborhood	0.0%	7.3%	0.0%	1.3%	17.2%
N =	(3)	(41)	(23)	(155)	(29)
Town or citywide	0.0%	12.5%	0.0%	3.1%	33.3%
N =	(3)	(48)	(112)	(163)	(3)

ry rates" according to hazard type and selected *household* characteristics. To illustrate, the first entry in the table, in the upper-left-hand corner, shows that there were, all told, 104 fire events in our data registered for households where the oldest member was less than 30 at the time of the event; and of these 104 events, 11.5% by the above definition resulted in injuries.

The general pattern found in Section A is that for fires, floods, and tornadoes, the youngest and oldest households were the most likely to sustain injuries of any kind. In the remaining hazards, hurricanes and earthquakes, households whose oldest members were over 65 years were the least likely to sustain any injury. Overall, the differences in Section A are quite small across the various age groups.

Section B considers differences with respect to the size of the household at the time of the event. No consistent patterns emerged: In general, large and small households were about equally likely to suffer an injury.

Section C considers differentials in injury by tenure. There was a slight tendency for owners in the cases of floods and tornadoes to sustain more injuries than renters. However, renters were more likely than owners to sustain injury as a result of hurricane events (4.1%). Here, too, the differences were quite small. The same holds for differences in injury rates by the race of the household head: No significant pattern can be found (Section D).

Section E shows differences in injury rates among the various income groups (household income as of the time of the event). In general, lower income households experienced higher rates of injuries than more affluent households. The difference was most pronounced in floods and earthquakes, where none of the higher income groups suffered any injury. Fires also showed a slight tendency for lower income households to suffer more injuries, but even here, the differences were not overwhelming.

In Section F, we made use of an index that we constructed to measure the context within which the event took place. The respondents were asked whether the damage due to the event was limited to their own homes or whether wider areas (other homes on the block, other homes in the neighborhood, or other homes in the city or town) were also affected. The index also provides a measure of whether the event was an isolated occurrence or whether the damages were spread over a larger area. Note first that *context*, as we have defined it, varied dramatically by type of hazard. Almost all fire events in our sample were isolated occurrences involving a single family, with only a very few affecting an entire block, neighborhood, or city. The same pattern holds for "earthquakes and earth tremors."[4] Floods, hurricanes, and tornadoes, in contrast, were much less likely to be single-family events and much more likely to affect whole areas of a community. Substantively, the general pattern is that injury rates are higher

---

[4]Earthquakes, of course, actually affect large areas. Our respondents apparently were indicating that theirs were the only homes affected to any apparent degree.

when damages occur over larger geographical areas. For example, in Section F under fires, we see that in isolated or single-family events, 8.6% resulted in injury, whereas in block fires, 23.5% of the events resulted in injury. This pattern holds across hazard types and is especially pronounced for earthquakes: When earthquake damages were spread widely over a city or town, injury occurred at a much higher rate (33%) than when damage was confined to only a single home (1%).

Table 5.6 shows a more sophisticated attempt to account for differences across households in the rate at which hazard-related injuries were sustained. The table shows the results of a multiple-regression analysis, where the dependent variable for the analysis was the total number of persons injured per 1,000 events and where the independent variables were the same household characteristics presented in Table 5.5. The cell entries show the regression coefficients (unstandardized) associated with each household characteristic, with their respective standard errors shown in parentheses below. At the bottom of the columns is the respective R^2 for each equation. The R^2 is a measure of the total variation in injuries per 1,000 events accounted for by the variables in the equation.

In the first column are the coefficients for fires. The coefficient for the age of the oldest household member indicates that for each one-year increase in the age of the oldest member, the number of persons injured per 1,000 events decreased by 1.36. Similarly, renters experienced 72 fewer injuries per 1,000 events than did owners. Magnitudes notwithstanding, neither of these coefficients is statistically distinguishable from zero.

In fact, it will be immediately noticed that very few of the regression coefficients in Table 5.6 are statistically significant. Furthermore, the R^2 values are very low and also not statistically significant (with one exception). Thus, we account for very little of the variation in injury with the household characteristics in these equations. Given that an event had been experienced, all families were about equally likely to incur an injury, regardless of the household's characteristics.

TABLE 5.6

Regression of Total Number of Persons Injured per 1,000 Events on Selected Household Characteristics (Dependent Variable Is Injuries[d] per 1,000 Households)

Independent variables	Fire b/SE	Flood b/SE	Hurricane b/SE	Tornado b/SE	Earthquake b/SE
Age of oldest member in household	-1.362 (2.40)	2.055 (3.13)	-.9318 (1.64)	1.798 (1.28)	-2.235 (2.21)
Size of household	-1.918 (22.6)	34.657 (31.06)	-2.480 (17.59)	-7.901 (13.16)	-4.379 (21.54)
Renter[a]	-72.15 (85.9)	-91.304 (100.3)	-19.908 (66.3)	-24.575 (55.1)	-102.379 (78.2)
White[b]	-6.959 (98.6)	-46.283 (182.1)	-65.577 (67.0)	-45.980 (76.9)	-201.96* (102.5)
Household income	-1.986 (3.27)	-9.739 (5.20)	-1.522 (2.20)	-1.869 (1.76)	-2.972 (2.78)
Context of disaster[c]	94.531 (125)	19.441 (102)	-68.88 (50.8)	25.828 (39.1)	232.42* (106)
Intercept	237.1 (171)	142.8 (253)	220.1 (118)	-26.65 (108)	400.8* (157)
$R^2 =$	.008	.043	.021	.011	.047*
$N =$	(209)	(116)	(204)	(470)	(281)

[a] Dummy variable: Deleted category is "owners."
[b] Dummy variable: Deleted category is "nonwhite households."
[c] Dummy variable: Deleted category is "isolated event."
[d] "Injury" includes death, physical illness, and "other injuries."
* $p < .05$

Earthquakes provide a partial exception. The R^2 value indicates that we can account for about 5% of the variation in injuries due to earthquakes, but the only significant coefficients are for race ($b = -202$) and disaster context ($b = 232$). Thus, nonwhites were somewhat more likely to be injured in an earthquake than whites, and areawide quakes caused more injury than localized events. These minor effects aside, however, the occurrence of injuries among household experiencing hazard events tended toward randomness. We cannot predict very accurately what kinds of households are likely to experience injuries using the variables in our equation.

"TOTAL DOLLAR COSTS" RESULTING FROM HAZARDS

Personal injury, of course, is only one of many sources of loss from a hazard event. As we have just seen, most hazard events are not accompanied by any injuries at all, some that are injurious are nonetheless minor, and many of the remainder generate relatively small medical-care costs (some portion of which, moreover, is usually defrayed by insurance). Thus, in estimating the total dollar costs associated with natural hazards, the direct medical-care costs incurred through personal injuries are, at best, a minor factor. In the present section, we consider the other components of total cost: The components due to loss of or damage to real and personal property.

The concern here is with "total dollar costs" due to the hazard event, as defined earlier in the chapter. These costs include the costs of medical care, damages to one's housing, any loss of valuables, the costs incurred in having to live in other places while repairs were made, wages lost through absence from work, and any and all other expenses incurred as a consequence of the hazard event.

The period between 1970 and 1980 was a highly inflationary one, prices rising almost 250%. Hence, in order to make damage experiences earlier in the period comparable with those of the later part of the period, we have adjusted all the damages to 1980 dollars. All of the tables presented in this section that contain dollar estimates have been so adjusted.

Obviously, total dollar costs can range from the trivial to the astronomical. In order to guage what, in general, were the total costs to a household as the aftermath of an event, we provide in Table 5.7 the average adjusted total dollar costs that resulted from having experienced a hazard event. As emphasized elsewhere, not all the events involved damages or losses. In the first row of the table, we report the percentages of events that were accompanied by no dollar costs whatsoever.[5] At one extreme are earthquake events, of which 88% involved no dollar costs at all. At the other extreme are fires and floods, where the majority of events were accompanied by dollar costs. Approximately 86% of all fire events and 76% of all flood events resulted in some dollar costs to the

[5]For purposes of the mail follow-up, hurricane, tornado, and earthquake events reported in the telephone screener interview as involving no damages or injuries were sampled at a lower rate than those events that involved either injury or damages (see Chapter 3). In order to correct the damage estimates contained in Table 5.7 (and all other tables in this chapter), we would ordinarily have compensated for this differential in sampling by weighting the number of cases reporting no damage or injuries in the mail survey by the inverse of their sampling fraction. For hurricanes and earthquakes, the weight to be applied was 1.34, and for tornadoes, 2.06. This weighting procedure would have produced the following results:

	Hurricanes	Tornadoes	Earthquakes
Number of cases in mail survey—unweighted	261	581	363
Weighted cases	298	784	469
Percentage of un- weighted cases with no damage	43.3	35.7	87.6
Percentage of weighted cases with no damage	50.6	52.7	90.5

The effect of weighting the cases in the analysis of the mail survey, then, is to reduce slightly the estimates of damage by increasing the number of no-damage events. We have not weighted the cases in this analysis because the bias introduced is small and in the direction of overestimating the damage estimates slightly.

household. Hurricanes and tornadoes are similar in the percentage of such events accompanied by no dollar costs (43% and 36%, respectively).

The second row of Section A shows the adjusted average total dollar costs sustained by households experiencing the various hazard events. Fires resulted in the highest average costs ($9,172) of all the hazard types. Floods also had high costs associated with them, $8,008 on average. Hurricanes and tornadoes produced similar average costs, $1,898 and $1,633, respectively. Earthquakes, with average total losses of only $322, were the least serious of all the hazards. These figures indicate that, on average, the dollar costs related to these events were by no means trivial. Of course, the actual costs varied dramatically around these averages, with a few high-loss families ("outliers") pulling the averages up. For this reason, the median cost figures, also presented in Section A, were in every case substantially lower. For example, we know that, on average, fires produced $9,172 in total costs, but the median dollar-cost figure indicates that 50% of all fire events resulted in total costs of less than $1,646. Half of all flood events resulted in less than $1,250 in losses. Similarly, hurricanes, tornadoes, and earthquakes produced substantially lower total losses than the mean amounts indicate. The pattern across hazard types, however, is the same with either measure.

A more informative way of analyzing the total dollar costs is to consider only those events involving at least some dollar costs. In Section B, we put aside all events that produced no costs at all and focus on the average and median costs for the remaining events. Of course, these estimates are higher, as expected. Over all fire events for which there were any costs, the average cost was $10,602; for analogous flood events, the average was $10,439. The median figures, also shown in Section B, indicate that among fire and flood events with any costs, half inflicted losses of less than $2,506 and $3,139, respectively. Although perhaps not devastating, these figures are assuredly not trivial.

Hurricanes and tornadoes, when they did cause losses, inflicted on average about the same amount, $3,317 and $2,541,

TABLE 5.7
Adjusted[a] Total Dollar Costs by Type of Hazard[b]

	Fire	Flood	Hurricane	Tornado	Earthquake
A. All incidents					
Percentage of events resulting in no dollar costs	13.5	23.3	43.3	35.7	87.6
Average adjusted dollar costs for all events	$9,172	$8,008	$1,898	$1,633	$322
Median adjusted dollar costs for all events	$1,646	$1,750	$ 77	$ 218	$ 0
N =	(252)	(146)	(254)	(568)	(355)
B. Incidents with non-zero damages					
Average adjusted dollar costs for events with costs	$10,602	$10,439	$3,347	$2,541	$2,001
Median adjusted dollar costs for events with costs	$ 2,506	$ 3,139	$ 795	$ 680	$1,000
N =	(218)	(112)	(114)	(365)	(44)

[a]All dollar estimates adjusted to 1980 price levels.
[b]This table is based on the unweighted event data; cf. footnote 5 in this chapter.

respectively. Again, the medians are lower. Of the hurricane events, 50% caused total dollar damages of less than $795; half of tornado events involved losses of less than $650. Although the majority of all the experienced earthquake events produced no costs, for those that did, the average amount of loss was $2,001, which is still the lowest amount shown for any hazard type. As for hurricanes and tornadoes, the median for cost-producing events was on the order of $1,000.

The evidence in Table 5.7 shows that the distribution of dollar loss from natural hazards was rather sharply skewed in two ways. First, some fraction of all the events inflicted no dollar costs at all; over hazard types, this fraction ranged from about 13.5% (fires) to 87.6% (earthquakes). And there is a further skew among those events causing at least some dollar damage, with catastrophic losses incurred by a few families raising the overall average substantially. To give a more direct sense of these loss distributions, Table 5.8 reports the distribution of loss over the five hazard types. For the purposes of this table, the total dollar costs have been classified into loss categories; the table then shows the distributions of events across these categories. These data reveal that 4.8% of fire events resulted in losses between $1 and $100, whereas less than 1% of flood and 1.7% of earthquake events resulted in total costs of that magnitude. Hurricanes and tornadoes had similar percentages of events within the $1–100 range (7.9% and 8.4%, respectively). Table 5.8 also indicates that most of the losses for all hazard events were within the $1–5,000 range. The percentage of catastrophic earthquake events, those resulting in more than $5,000 in costs, was very small, about 2%. The same was true of hurricanes (8.7%) and tornadoes (6.5%). However, such was not the case for fires and floods. One-quarter of these events resulted in total costs of more than $5,000 (31.4% and 29.5%, respectively). Fire events were much more likely to cause catastrophic losses, as indicated by the 16.7% of such events resulting in costs of over $20,000. Floods were less likely to result in

TABLE 5.8

Distribution of Adjusted[a] Total Dollar Cost by Type of Hazard
(Total Dollar Cost Corrected for Inflation to 1980 Dollars)

Adjusted cost (dollars)	Fires Percent	Floods Percent	Hurricanes Percent	Tornadoes Percent	Earthquakes Percent
0	13.5	23.3	43.3	35.7	87.6
1–$100	4.8	0.7	7.9	8.4	1.7
101–$500	11.1	7.5	14.2	18.8	2.8
501–$2,000	23.0	24.0	18.5	21.6	3.9
2,001–$5,000	16.3	15.1	7.5	8.8	2.0
5,001–$10,000	7.1	6.2	3.9	3.5	1.1
10,001–$15,000	4.8	4.8	2.4	1.0	0.6
15,001–$20,000	2.8	4.1	0.0	0.2	0.0
20,001 or more	16.7	14.4	2.4	1.8	0.3
N =	(252)	(146)	(254)	(568)	(355)

[a]Estimates adjusted to 1980 dollars.

such high costs; however, a substantial percentage (14.4%) inflicted losses over $20,000. The high average total-dollar costs presented in Table 5.7 for fires and floods are due mainly to the large proportion that caused truly catastrophic damages.

NATIONAL ESTIMATES OF TOTAL DOLLAR COSTS

The design of the research reported permits projections of total dollar costs to the national level. The telephone survey reported in the previous chapter provided estimates of the number of households that suffered nontrivial losses, and the average losses are shown in Table 5.7. Multiplying these two sets of numbers yields the national estimates shown in Table 5.9.

Note that these estimates pertain only to the total costs of damages borne by households. Natural hazards also inflict damages on business and public entities, none of which are allocated to households. Hence, the estimates given in Table 5.9 are not inclusive of all damages, but only of those borne directly by households through injuries to members or damages to real and personal property held by household members.

In addition, these are adjusted annualized estimates, meaning

TABLE 5.9
*National Annualized Adjusted[a] Estimates[b] of Total Household Costs
Inflicted by Natural Hazard Events*

Hazard	Adjusted[a] national annual estimates[b]
Household fires	$4,600,000,000
Floods	2,800,000,000
Hurricanes and severe tropical storms	900,000,000
Tornadoes and severe windstorms	2,000,000,000
Earthquakes and tremors	400,000,000
Total of all five above	$10.7 billion
Total of four natural hazards	$ 6.1 billion

[a]Adjusted to 1980 dollars.
[b]Computed by projecting adjusted total dollar costs, as obtained from mail survey, to incidence rates (see Chapter 4), as obtained from the telephone screening interviews.

that they have been inflated to 1980 dollars and constitute the average annual household costs for the 11-year period 1970 through 1980.

Household fires were clearly the most costly hazard studied, producing an annual $4.6 billion in damages to households. Floods were next in importance with $2.8 billion, followed rather closely by tornadoes and severe windstorms ($2.0 billion), with hurricanes and earthquakes trailing quite far behind ($.9 billion and $.4 billion, respectively). Added together, the five hazard damages totaled $10.7 billion annually, with the four natural hazards totaling $6.1 billion.

Note that these estimates are close to those given by hazards specialists as discussed in Chapter 2 (and in Appendix A) for all hazard damages combined, including hazards not studied in this research and including damages to business enterprises and public bodies. Hence, the estimates in Table 5.9 appear to be on the high side, possibly expressing the known bias in our surveys toward higher rates of response from households that had experienced greater amounts of damage (as discussed in Chapter 3). In addition, these estimates may also reflect the possibility that there are categories of damages that were not reflected directly in the sources from which other estimates were made. Thus, there may be costs that are directly absorbed by households that do not lead to loans from federal sources, gifts from friends and relatives, and so on that cover the losses inflicted by natural hazards. Such sources are explored in some detail in Chapter 6.

In any event, the annual losses from these four natural hazards are considerable, constituting a heavy burden for afflicted households. This assessment stands, whether the total annual average burden is $4 billion, $6 billion, or $8 billion.

DAMAGE TO PROPERTY AND PERSONAL POSSESSIONS

The data just discussed summarize total dollar costs to households resulting from hazard events. Even at the averages, the total costs are likely to have direct and negative consequences for a family's economic well-being: For households suffering any dollar loss, the average losses often run into the hundreds, or even thousands, of dollars; and for a sizable fraction of flood and fire victims, at least into the tens of thousands of dollars. These dollar losses, of course, have several components—medical costs, lost wages, and so on—but as we shall see in the present section, the major component by far is damage to homes and personal property.

As every home owner knows, dollar damages to a home can rapidly mount. A foot or so of flood water in one's basement would not normally constitute a major catastrophe, but if, as is often the case, there is a furnace, a water heater, a washer and dryer, or other similar appliances located there, the ensuing damages could easily add up to several thousands of dollars. Likewise, a kitchen fire that destroys a major appliance can become a serious expense for the household. Because damages to property and personal possessions are often the major component of total costs, we address the topic of property damages in some detail in this section. Specifically, we examine the kinds of things that are damaged as a result of a hazard event and the costs of replacing or restoring them.

We asked respondents, "Did you or your family or household suffer any damages to your house or apartment or damages to your furniture or personal property as a result of the event?" The findings in this section are limited to only those households that answered "Yes." Households answering "Yes" were then asked whether each of 18 items was damaged as a result of the event and what the amount of damage to the item was. To facilitate the analysis, we have grouped these items into six categories of damage, as follows:

1. Structural damage
   Includes damage to the following:
   1. Roof on building
   2. Basement or foundation
   3. Walls or floors

    4. Windows or doors

    5. Furnace, air conditioners, or hot water heater

2. External damages

   Includes damage to the following:

    1. Yard or landscaping

    2. Garage or other building on property

    3. Other part of building

3. Furniture damage

   Includes damage to the following:

    1. Furniture

    2. Rugs or curtains

    3. Appliances

4. Clothing damage

   Includes damage to the following:

    1. Clothing only

5. Personal-item damage

   Includes damage to the following:

    1. Books or papers

    2. Radio, TV, or stereo

    3. Jewelry

6. All other damage

   Includes damage to the following:

    1. Pets

    2. Cars, trucks, or other vehicles

    3. Any other personal property

The original list of 18 items captures most of the kinds of things that can be damaged as a result of a hazard event. The six constructed categories attempt to group together items that constitute similar kinds of damages. For example, damage to structure includes any damage to the roof of the building, the basement or foundation, the walls or floors, windows or door, or to the furnace or hot water heater. When we speak of damage to structure, then, we are referring to damages involving any one or some combination of these five items. Also, for each of the six categories, the sum of the dollar damage for each of the items comprising the group gives us a total dollar damage estimate for that category. (If an item in the category was not damaged, we added $0 to the category total when computing that total.) Data are shown in Table 5.10.

The first row of the table shows the percentage of events that caused any damage to property and other personal possessions. The percentages mirror those in Table 5.7, showing the percentages of events accompanied by any costs. For example, 85.7% of all fire events involved at least some damage to property and possessions. A little more than three-quarters (76.4%) of all floods and about two-thirds of all tornadoes (64.8%) resulted in property damages. A slight majority of households experiencing hurricane events suffered such damages (55.2%), but only a small minority of earthquake events (14.4%) resulted in any kind of property damage. *In all the remaining panels of Table 5.10, the percentages shown are based on only those events that resulted in at least some damage to property or personal possessions.* For convenience, we refer to these as *damaging events.*

Section B shows the percentage of damaging events that resulted in damage to structural features. By and large, structural damages accounted for the bulk of total dollar costs, as shown later. A large majority of all damaging events inflicted some structural damage, the proportions ranging upward of two-thirds for all hazard types.

Although a large majority of damaging hazard events inflicted some kind of structural damage, the average amount of damage varied across hazard types. On average, fire and flood events produced the highest average amounts of dollar damage to structure ($2,409 and $2,395, respectively). Hurricanes, on the other hand, produced less damage on average ($1,447) as did tornadoes ($1,081) and earthquakes ($1,595). Also contained in Section B are the median damage costs. That figure indicates that for fire and flood events resulting in property damage, 50% of the events produced structural damages of $500 or less, and that 50% of the remaining hazard events produced less than $300 in such damages.

TABLE 5.10
Adjusted[a] Dollar Damages by Damage Categories for Events Causing
Any Damages to Property and Possessions

Category of damage	Fire	Flood	Hurricane	Tornado	Earthquake
Section A					
Percentage of events causing damage to property and possessions	85.7	76.4	55.2	64.8	14.4
N =	(266)	(148)	(259)	(580)	(354)
Section B					
Percentage of events with structural damage[b]	82.7	76.1	71.1	67.9	76.5
Average adjusted damage	$2,409	$2,395	$1,447	$1,081	$1,595
Median adjusted damage	$ 442	$ 454	$ 204	$ 148	$ 318
For those with structural damage					
Average	$3,144	$3,406	$2,170	$1,673	$2,212
Median	$ 935	$1,075	$ 632	$ 555	$ 651
Section C					
Percentage of events with external damages[c]	34.7	56.6	75.4	63.6	31.4
Average adjusted damage	$1,139	$ 906	$ 633	$ 582	$ 315
Median adjusted damage	$ 1	$ 0	$ 225	$ 85	$ 2
For those with external damages					
Average	$5,430	$1,915	$ 900	$1,007	$1,318
Median	$1,576	$ 501	$ 350	$ 300	$ 998
Section D					
Percentage of events with furniture damage[d]	76.4	66.4	24.6	12.3	19.6
Average adjusted damage	$2,031	$1,956	$ 341	$ 46	$ 93
Median adjusted damage	$ 334	$ 172	$ 0	$ 0	$ 8
For those with furniture damage					
Average	$2,936	$3,237	$1,802	$ 433	$ 511
Median	$ 900	$ 835	$ 507	$ 292	$ 394

(continued)

TABLE 5.10   (Continued)

Category of damage	Fire	Flood	Hurricane	Tornado	Earthquake
Section E					
Percentage of events with clothing damage[e]	46.7	45.1	9.9	2.1	2.0
Average adjusted damage	$ 696	$ 415	$ 143	$ 2	f
Median adjusted damage	$ 0	$ 1	$ 2	$ 0	f
For those with clothing damage					
Average	$2,065	$1,171	$2,434	$ 186	f
Median	$ 632	$ 569	$ 630	$ 70	f
Section F					
Percentage of events with personal item damage[g]	40.0	48.7	11.2	8.6	17.6
Average adjusted damage	$ 476	$ 456	$ 106	$ 22	$ 48
Median adjusted damage	$ 1	$ 2	$ 0	$ 0	$ 3
For those with personal item damage					
Average	$1,814	$1,035	$1,589	$ 305	$ 338
Median	$ 724	$ 379	$ 253	$ 170	$ 376
Section G					
Percentage of events with other damage[h]	29.3	48.7	26.1	27.0	41.2
Average adjusted damage	$ 511	$1,059	$ 274	$ 442	$ 159
Median adjusted damage	$ 0	$ 0	$ 0	$ 0	$ 1
For those with other damage					
Average	$2,444	$2,488	$1,147	$1,831	$ 424
Median	$ 788	$ 632	$ 400	$ 492	$ 108
Base N^i =	(225)	(113)	(142)	(374)	(51)

[a]Adjusted to 1980 Dollars.
[b]Components of structural damage are roof on building; basement or foundation; walls or floors; windows or doors; furnace, air conditioner, or hot water heater.
[c]Components of external damage are yard or landscaping; garage or other building on property; other part of building.
[d]Components of furniture damage are furniture; rugs or curtains; appliances.
[e]Components of clothing damage are clothing.
[f]Number of cases in cell (N = 1) too small to allow computation of statistics.
[g]Components of personal-item damage are books or papers; radio, TV, or stereo; jewelry.
[h]Components of other damage are pets; cars or trucks; any other personal property.
[i]Base N is the number of events that had damage to property or personal possessions. The base number fluctuates slightly in the calculations because of some missing data.

The last two rows of Section B focus on only those damaging events that resulted in at least some structural damages. The averages, of course, increase. For structurally damaging fire and flood events, the average damages were $3,144 and $3,406, respectively. As in all other cases, the median dollar damages are lower. Structurally damaging hurricane, tornado, and earthquake events caused less damage than either fire or flood events. On average, hurricanes resulted in $2,170 in damages, and tornadoes and earthquakes averaged $1,673 and $2,212, respectively, in damages, with medians beneath $1,000 in each case.

Section C shows the percentage of damaging events that caused exterior damage. As might be expected, fires and earthquakes were much more likely to cause structural damage than exterior damage, about one-third of them resulting in damages to external items. Damages to the exterior were higher for floods (57%) than for either fires or earthquakes, and higher still for tornadoes (64%) and hurricanes (75%). All these patterns are as one would expect, given the nature of the hazards.

In general, losses due to exterior damage were considerably less than losses due to structural damage. On average, fire events produced $1,139 in damages to external items; floods, $906; hurricanes, $633; tornadoes, $582; and earthquakes, $315. If the analysis is restricted only to damaging events causing at least some exterior damage, all the averages rise. To illustrate, over all damaging fires, the average external damage done amounted to about $1,100. However, only about 35% of all "damaging fires" caused any exterior damage, and among those that did, the average exterior damage done amounted to nearly $5,430. Similar—although less pronounced—patterns are evident for the other hazard types.

Section D shows the percentage of events resulting in damage to household furnishings. Households experiencing damage from fires or floods were very likely to suffer furniture damages, over three-fourths of them in fire events and about two-thirds in flood events. On average, the amounts of damage sustained were also quite high. In the case of damaging fires, the average furniture damage was $2,031, and for flood events, $1,956. About 25% of hurricane and 20% of earthquake events cause furniture damage, and the average amount of damage was relatively low. Tornadoes were the least likely of the hazards to produce damage to furniture (12.3%), and the average amount of damage was also low.

As indicated in Section E, damage to clothing was rare in hurricane, tornado, and earthquake events, and rather common in fires and floods (about one-half of these latter causing at least some damage to clothing). In events where clothing was damaged, however, the replacement costs were rather high, averaging (as an example) $2,065 in the case of fire, and $1,171 in the case of floods. (The average for hurricanes is based on only one or two cases and is therefore unreliable.)

Section F shows the percentage of damaging events that caused damages to personal possessions (other than furniture or clothing). Almost 50% of the damaging flood events and about 40% of the damaging fires resulted in some damage to personal items. The average amounts of damage to such items were small compared with other kinds of losses (about $400–500 on average); however, when singling out only those events that actually produced damage to personal items, the average amounts again increased markedly. Personal items were damaged infrequently in the remaining types of hazards.

Section G shows the percentage of events resulting in damages to "other" items, mainly cars and trucks. This appears to be a relatively important source of loss in some hazards: primarily in floods, to a lesser degree in tornadoes and hurricanes, and relatively unimportantly in the other types of events. To illustrate, about one-half of the damaging floods represented in these data caused damages in the "other" category, and the average loss inflicted as a result was higher than the average loss to either personal possessions or clothing.

Summarizing briefly, Table 5.10 gives estimates of both the types of property that are damaged and the average amounts of such damages. Fires are most likely to cause serious damages to structural items, furniture, and clothing. Floods, on the other hand, are likely to result in damage not only to structural, furniture, and clothing items but to all other damage categories as well. The lower total dollar costs reported for floods in Table 5.7 obviously imply not that fewer or different kinds of items are damaged in floods relative to fires, but that fire tends to destroy what floods tend only to damage. Hurricanes and tornadoes show some similarity in the kinds of damages they produce. Both of these hazards involve high winds and rains, and the kinds of damages sustained during these events reflect this. For example, both result in damages to a combination of structural and external items much more often than do any of the other hazards; however, they are less likely to cause damage to either clothing or furniture. Also, in both these hazards, items classified under "other" are likely to be damaged in about one-quarter of such events. Earthquakes, on the other hand, are most likely to produce damages to the structural items and to items classified under "other."

Table 5.10 provides estimates of how frequently various types of damages occur and what the average damages are. However, these findings do not allow us, in any direct fashion, to gauge the importance of property damage in the "total dollar costs" accompanying the event. Specifically, how much of the total cost accompanying an event is represented by property damage? What percentage of the total cost is accounted for by damage to the 18 items that comprise our six damage categories, as well as the six categories themselves?

Table 5.11 shows the percentage of "total dollar costs" accounted for by each of the 18 loss categories. These percentages were calculated by dividing the various amounts of category-specific damage by the total dollar costs of the event. Data are shown for damaging events only, as defined earlier.

For example, in the bottom row of Table 5.11, we find that on average, 87.5% of the total dollar costs of a damaging fire event was accounted for by property damage. The percentages across hazard types range upward from 90%. In the case of damaging hurricanes and tornadoes, virtually all costs were due to property damages, whereas in earthquakes the percentage was 93%, and in

TABLE 5.11
Percentage of "Total Dollar Costs" Accounted for by Components of Property Damage for Those Events Causing Property Damage by Type of Hazard

Components	Fire	Flood	Hurricane	Tornado	Earthquake
Structural items					
Roof on building	2.7	3.4	22.7	31.1	3.7
Basement/foundation	1.9	8.2	1.9	0.5	14.1
Walls or floors	28.6	9.8	4.2	3.7	25.0
Windows or doors	1.4	1.7	6.0	9.2	8.6
Furnace, air conditioners, or hot water heater	2.2	6.8	3.3	0.5	1.2
Structural damages[a]	38.5	30.8	39.6	45.5	54.8
External items					
Yard/landscaping	1.0	9.4	30.0	31.9	11.3
Garage/other building	1.9	3.3	4.1	8.9	1.7
Other part of building	4.9	1.4	5.1	6.1	1.1
External damages[a]	8.5	14.9	40.6	33.7	7.9
Furniture items					
Furniture	9.3	9.3	1.2	0.7	2.2
Rugs or curtains	7.7	5.2	2.6	1.1	0.4
Appliances	9.6	6.3	1.1	0.2	0.1
Furniture damages[a]	28.1	21.2	5.1	2.1	2.9

(continued)

floods, 90%. Thus, property damage is unquestionably the major source of dollar loss from natural hazards.

There are interesting differences across hazard types in the patterns of damages to property. In terms of percentage shares of the total dollar losses, fire damages tended to be concentrated on the floors and the walls of the structure, and on household furnishings. No other single category of property damage accounted for more than about 5% of the total dollar loss in damaging fires. Flood damages were, in contrast, far more diffuse, with no single category accounting for a greatly disproportionate share. Hurricane and tornado damages followed a very similar pattern, with over one-half of the total dollar loss from both kinds of events being concentrated in only two categories: the roof and the yard.

TABLE 5.11   (Continued)

Components	Fire	Flood	Hurricane	Tornado	Earthquake
Clothing items					
Clothing	5.1	4.2	1.1	0.1	0.0
Clothing damage	5.1	4.2	1.1	0.1	0.0
Personal items					
Books or papers	1.0	2.7	0.7	0.1	1.2
Radio, TV, or stereo	1.6	1.7	0.8	2.6	3.0
Jewelry	0.2	0.1	0.1	0.0	0.0
Personal-item damage[a]	3.1	4.5	1.7	2.8	4.4
Other items					
Pets	0.3	0.0	0.0	0.0	0.0
Cars, trucks, or vehicles	0.2	8.0	2.6	7.0	0.0
Any other personal property	3.6	6.0	6.3	5.8	22.0
Other item damage[a]	4.2	14.6	9.2	13.2	23.0
Percentage of "total dollar cost" accounted for by damage to property	87.5	90.2	97.3	97.4	93.0
N^b =	(225)	(113)	(142)	(374)	(51)

[a]The sum of the percentages of "total dollar costs" accounted for by individual items is not equal to the percentage of "total dollar costs" accounted for by the damage category as a whole. The slight difference is due to the way the percentages were calculated. In calculating the percentage of total dollar costs accounted for by individual items, items with missing data were deleted from the calculation; however, the percentage of total dollar cost accounted for by the damage category was calculated even if one or two items contained missing information.
[b]Base fluctuates slightly because of missing data.

Like flood damages, earthquake damages tended to be rather diffuse, with structural damages, especially to walls, floor, foundation, or basement, accounting for the largest aggregate share.

THE DISTRIBUTION OF DOLLAR COSTS BY HOUSEHOLD CHARACTERISTICS

The analyses reported to this point give some indication of the magnitude of losses associated with hazard events, but not of how these losses tend to vary as a function of household characteristics. Are some families more prone to suffer property damages in a hazard event than others? As an initial approach to this question, Table 5.12 shows the proportion of families suffering any dollar loss from their hazard event as this proportion varies over (1) hazard types and (2) the characteristics of the household. To illustrate, the first entry in the table shows that there were 99 fire events in our sample occurring to households where the oldest member was younger than 30, and of these 99 events, 81.8% caused at least some dollar damages.

Section A shows differences across households by the age of the oldest member. Overall, the youngest households were the least likely to sustain any losses, and households with their oldest members in the 31- to 44-year-old range were generally the most likely to sustain losses. Only in the case of earthquakes were the very youngest households more likely to suffer losses (13.8%) than other age groups. For fires, about 82% of households with the oldest member under age 30 incurred any losses; in contrast, households in the 31–44 age group had 88% suffering losses, and for those in the 65 and over category, 100% suffered losses. The same pattern held true in the cases of hurricanes and tornadoes: Households in the 31–44 and the 65 and over groups had the highest loss rates. In floods, however, the two middle-aged groups most often suffered losses.

Section B shows differences with respect to the size of the household at the time of the event. There are no sharp patterns that hold across disaster types. Hurricane loss tended to increase rather sharply with household size. Single-person households were distinctly less likely than others to incur loss in a flood, whereas the same households were more likely than others to sustain a loss in fires. With the exception of the hurricane result, none of these patterns is pronounced.

Section C shows differences according to the race of the household head. Floods showed a marked difference in the rates of sustaining costs between whites (80%) and minorities (100%), but the nonwhite N was very small. An equally sharp difference is

TABLE 5.12

Percentages of Households, by Selected Characteristics, Sustaining Any Dollar Costs by Type of Hazard

Selected characteristic	Fire	Flood	Hurricane	Tornado	Earthquake
Section A					
Age of oldest person in household at time of event					
Under 30 years	81.8%	64.8%	46.2%	64.2%	13.8%
	(99)	(71)	(78)	(201)	(138)
31–44 years	88.3%	96.8%	65.1%	65.2%	13.1%
	(77)	(31)	(86)	(187)	(99)
45–64 years	87.7%	88.2%	58.7%	61.5%	13.1%
	(57)	(34)	(63)	(135)	(84)
65 and over	100.0%	71.4%	64.7%	73.7%	6.7%
	(16)	(7)	(17)	(38)	(15)
Section B					
Size of household at time of event					
1 person	91.7%	55.6%	33.3%	61.2%	14.8%
	(12)	(18)	(21)	(67)	(54)
2 persons	84.9%	78.1%	45.4%	68.0%	12.0%
	(53)	(32)	(66)	(122)	(83)
3–5 persons	87.1%	90.3%	60.1%	64.1%	9.9%
	(147)	(62)	(141)	(309)	(171)
6+ persons	84.6%	85.7%	100.0%	62.5%	16.7%
	(26)	(14)	(13)	(32)	(18)
Section C					
Race					
White	87.3%	80.2%	57.0%	65.9%	12.2%
	(205)	(121)	(200)	(501)	(296)
Minority	85.3%	100.0%	53.7%	41.7%	13.9%
	(34)	(10)	(41)	(36)	(36)
Section D					
Tenure					
Rent	79.7%	74.7%	34.7%	47.4%	8.3%
	(64)	(39)	(49)	(95)	(96)
Own	88.5%	79.2%	61.6%	68.9%	14.4%
	(182)	(101)	(203)	(456)	(243)

(continued)

TABLE 5.12   (Continued)

Selected characteristic	Fire	Flood	Hurricane	Tornado	Earthquake
Section E Household income at time of event					
Under $10,000	96.7%	78.1%	40.0%	58.5%	16.4%
	(61)	(32)	(40)	(94)	(61)
$10,000–$15,000	87.5%	85.7%	64.3%	61.5%	12.5%
	(56)	(35)	(42)	(104)	(48)
$15,000–$20,000	88.0%	85.7%	66.7%	66.7%	8.0%
	(25)	(21)	(30)	(84)	(50)
$20,000–$25,000	81.0%	81.2%	72.7%	57.1%	2.5%
	(21)	(16)	(33)	(70)	(40)
$25,000–$40,000	91.7%	100.0%	50.0%	70.0%	21.4%
	(12)	(6)	(18)	(40)	(28)
Section F Seriousness of disaster context					
Isolated	85.2%	49.0%	22.9%	38.5%	6.2%
	(230)	(49)	(109)	(221)	(320)
Block	100.0%	82.6%	66.7%	69.6%	70.0%
	(20)	(23)	(36)	(125)	(10)
Neighborhood	a	94.9%	80.6%	86.6%	66.7%
		(39)	(36)	(127)	(24)
City or town	100.0%	91.4%	90.4%	87.4%	100.0%
	(2)	(35)	(73)	(95)	(1)

a No cases in cell.

also evident in the case of tornadoes, but in the opposite direction. For the remaining hazards, there are no real differences between white and minority households.

Section D shows differences by tenure. Overall, renters were less likely than owners to suffer any costs, across all hazard types. The difference between renters and owners was more pronounced for hurricanes, tornadoes, and earthquakes than for the remaining hazard types.

Differences among income groups were mixed and generally weak (Section E). In fires, the lowest income groups suffered losses most often (96.7%), followed by those in the over-$40,000 group (91.7%); however, the loss rate was quite high across all income categories. In the case of floods, the lowest income groups had the lowest rate (78.1%), and those in the over-$40,000 group had the highest rate (100%). In both hurricanes and tornadoes, the lowest income groups were the least likely to have had any costs, whereas in earthquakes, the highest income group had the largest proportion with losses.

Section F shows loss rates by disaster context, as defined earlier. The general pattern is that the more widespread the damages, the more likely the increase in household losses. This pattern is most pronounced in the case of earthquakes.

Table 5.12 treats loss as an "either-or" condition: Either a family suffered at least some dollar loss, or it did not. The "total dollar loss" is obviously a more sensitive measure. Table 5.13 shows the multiple regression of total dollar loss for selected household characteristics. As in the earlier regression, the entries give the unstandardized regression coefficients associated with each independent variable; these are readily interpreted as the increase (or decrease) in predicted total dollar losses due to a unit increase in the corresponding independent variable. The standard errors of estimate are reported in parentheses beneath each coefficient; the R^2 values are measures of how well were dollar losses predicted by the characteristics in the equation.

The high R^2 values for floods ($R^2 = .314$) and earthquakes ($R^2 = .305$) indicate that we do best in predicting total dollar costs for these two events. In the case of floods, household size, tenure, household income, and disaster context were the significant predictors of total dollar costs. Knowing that a household rented— rather than owned—its home would lead us to predict total losses of $6,048 less. Similarly, for every $1,000 increase in household income, we would predict approximately $529 less in total costs. Every unit increase in our context variable (knowing that damage was not an isolated occurrence) led to a $5,228 expected increase in total costs.

Although the R^2 is almost as high in the case of earthquakes, the only significant predictor of total cost was the context within

TABLE 5.13

Regression of Adjusted[a] Total Dollar Costs on Selected Household Characteristics
(Dependent Variable Is Adjusted[a] Total Dollar Cost)

	Fires	Floods	Hurricanes	Tornadoes	Earthquakes
	b/SE	b/SE	b/SE	b/SE	b/SE
Age of oldest person in household	-35.49	63.54	2.44	-36.44*	-9.59
	(73.5)	(70.2)	(27.2)	(17.4)	(6.1)
Size of household	1,093	1,565*	587*	277	-89
	(688)	(695)	(296)	(179)	(59)
White[b]	-3,630	745	128	840	107
	(3,006)	(4,073)	(1,107)	(1,045)	(281)
Renter[c]	-6,427*	-6,048*	472	-1,482	-210
	(2,594)	(2,486)	(1,099)	(751)	(214)
Household income (thousands of dollars)	-102	-529***	-26	-53	-8
	(83)	(117)	(36)	(24)	(8)
Seriousness of disaster context	3,336	5,228***	1,310***	703**	1,680***
	(2,887)	(919)	(333)	(232)	(163)
Intercept	12,906*	2,526	-1,472	1,851	529
	(5,184)	(5,528)	(1,956)	(1,475)	(431)
R² =	.061*	.314***	.110***	.044**	.305***
N =	(209)	(116)	(204)	(470)	(281)

[a]Adjusted to 1980 dollars.
[b]Dummy variable: Omitted category is "nonwhite."
[c]Dummy variable: Omitted category is "owners."

  *p < .05
 **p < .01
***p < .001

which the event took place. For every one-unit increase in our context index, we would expect a $168 increase in total dollar losses.

The R^2's for the remaining hazards are all statistically significant but also relatively small, ranging from .04 to about .11. In the case of fires, tenure was the only significant predictor of total loss. There were no differences in total loss by age, race, or income. For hurricanes, with every additional person in the household, we expect a $587 increase in total costs. In addition, knowing that damage was not limited to their home alone leads us to predict an increase of $1,310 in losses. Finally, we do best in predicting losses from tornadoes when we know the age of the oldest person in the household, tenure, household income, and the disaster context.

SUMMARY

The untoward *sequelae* of natural hazards include, but are assuredly not limited to, deaths, injuries, and dollar damages. In general, as others have remarked, death has become a rather uncommon consequence of natural hazards, no doubt owing in large measure to the very impressive improvements in warning systems that have developed during the past few decades, and perhaps to improvements in emergency medical care and in the hazard safety of dwellings as well. In our data, personal injury was also relatively rare, occurring in fewer than one-tenth of all events. Further, most of the medical care costs incurred as a result of these events were modest in dollar terms.

Measured in terms of direct dollar cost, property loss is by far the most common source of loss from a hazard event, with average dollar costs running into the hundreds and even thousands of dollars. As would be expected, most of these costs are accounted for by damage to residences or to their contents. The numbers reported in this chapter strongly suggest that many families would find it extremely difficult to cope with the economic consequences of a hazard event were they left entirely on their own. But it is also well known that many, perhaps most, hazard-victimized familes are not left to their own devices. On the contrary, many sources of external aid often become available to them, whether this aid comes in the form of insurance coverage, governmental relief and rehabilitation funds, local community support, or the generously shared resources of family and friends. Indeed, the "cost accounting" provided in this chapter totes up only the loss side of the ledger; a complete accounting would have to include not only the losses incurred but also the assistance received. And that is the topic of the following chapter.

CHAPTER 6

Patterns of Aid to Hazard Victims

INTRODUCTION

Although no amount of aid, financial or otherwise, can completely compensate for all the consequences of a major trauma, the restoration of the *status quo ante* can be aided considerably by various kinds of help. The sources of help and the extent to which they affect the household's return to normality are the subjects of this chapter. We consider such diverse sources of aid as insurance payments, gifts, and loans, as well as help in goods or services rendered by relatives, friends, and neighbors.

A critical issue in the analysis is the extent to which aid reaches impacted households in an equitable way. In this connection, there are two main questions to be raised. First, how large a proportion of the households in need are reached by the agencies that provide aid to stricken households? Second, is aid distributed equitably among households that vary by socioeconomic level, tenure, age, race, and other characteristics? A final topic dealt with here concerns the speed with which households are restored to their "normal" prehazard condition. What affects the time it takes to restore normality?

A Technical Note

Throughout this chapter, we distinguish usually between "serious" events and "minor" ones, based mainly on the amount of damages or the number of injuries suffered by households. However, this distinction, for good reason, is not always followed, and all events, regardless of amount of damage or number of injuries, are considered one group for some analyses. The reader is urged to note the headings of the tables, in which the kinds of households used in the tabulations are described.

Insurance Coverage and Claims

Although almost all home-owner insurance policies cover losses from fires and most cover damages from windstorms, coverage of flood and earthquake hazards is neither usual nor frequent. In addition, a large proportion of renters and some owners do not have property insurance at all.[1] Even in communities in which flood insurance subsidized under the National Flood Insurance Program is available, coverage is voluntary and many opt not to be covered. In states such as California, where earthquake risk coverage is available and offered routinely by insurers, only small proportions elect to be covered (Kunreuther et al., 1977).

In Table 6.1, the insurance experiences of all households that had suffered damages of any magnitude are shown. Section A shows the percentages of households that believed at the time of the event that they had insurance to cover the losses sustained.

---

[1]Among renters who had experienced some dollar damages, 31% thought that their insurance would cover their losses. In contrast, 81% of owning households believed that they had insurance coverage for their losses. Of course, perceived insurance coverage varied widely by type of hazard experience: At one extreme, 92% of the home owners believed that their insurance would cover damages received from fires; at the other extreme, 70% of the renters believed that their insurance would not cover earthquake damages.

Percentages are shown separately for events that caused $50 or more in damages (serious experiences) and those that caused less damage (minor experiences). As might be expected, strong majorities of households experiencing serious fires (83%), hurricane damage (82%), and tornado damage (81%) expected that their insurance would cover at least some portion of their losses. The corresponding proportions for floods and earthquakes were much lower (45% and 35%, respectively). Note that because some of the damage losses were incurred through injuries and might have been covered by medical and/or surgical policies, the inflicted costs might well have been covered even though property insurance policies excluded property damages from the hazard in question.

The percentages filing claims (as shown in Section B) tended to follow the same pattern noted above. Claim filings were more frequent among those suffering from serious fires (93%), hurricanes (77%), and tornadoes (80%). Fewer claims were filed for floods (65%) or earthquakes (38%). In addition, claims were less frequently filed for minor losses (less than $50) under all hazard conditions.

The patterning of differences among hazard types is again repeated when we consider whether a claim was honored (Section C). Virtually all serious fire claims were honored (99%), and close to all of the tornado (94%) and hurricane claims (89%) were also honored. Three out of four (77%) flood claims and a few more than one out of three (38%) earthquake claims were met with some payment.

If we multiply through the various probabilities displayed in Table 6.1, we obtain the following proportions of serious hazard events for which some kind of insurance payment was made[2]:

---

[2]For example, the percentage of all serious fires receiving payment is the product of the proportion believing they were covered, the proportion who submitted claims, and the proportion receiving claims (.83 × .93 × .99 = .76, or 76%). No calculations for minor hazard events were made because of the small numbers of such events.

TABLE 6.1
Insurance Experiences Connected with Hazard Victimization[a]
(Only Households with Nonzero Dollar Damages Hazard Event)

Hazard seriousness[b]	Fire	Flood	Hurricane	Tornado	Earthquake
A. Believed damage was covered by insurance (percent)					
Serious	83	45	82	81	35
N =	(213)	(108)	(125)	(324)	(37)
Minor	30	c	88	53	60
N =	(10)	(1)	(16)	(32)	(5)
B. Filed a claim for damage (percent)[d]					
Serious	93	65	77	80	38
N =	(178)	(49)	(102)	(264)	(13)
Minor	67	c	7	12	0
N =	(3)	(1)	(14)	(17)	(3)
C. Claim honored (percent)[e]					
Serious	99	77	89	94	60
N =	(165)	(31)	(78)	(210)	(5)
Minor	c	c	c	c	c
N =	(2)	(1)	(1)	(1)	(1)

D. Treated fairly by insurance company (percent)[e]					
Very fair	67	39	56	71	20
Somewhat fair	15	29	13	18	40
Somewhat unfair	11	16	23	7	0
Very unfair	6	15	8	3	40
N =	(164)	(31)	(75)	(207)	(5)
E. Complaints about insurance company (percent)[f]					
Payment slow	39	33	52	20	0
Disallow unfairly	27	56	48	43	50
Payment too small	67	40	68	60	0
Bad manners	15	11	22	18	0
N =	(33)	(9)	(23)	(28)	(12)

[a] See questionnaire in Appendix B for exact wording of questions. Table covers only households with nonzero dollar damages (property losses or medical expenses).

[b] Minor events involved neither damages over $50 nor medical expenses. Serious events include all others (damages over $50 and/or injuries and/or evacuation). Damages are not corrected for inflation.

[c] Number answering too small (under 4) to compute percentages.

[d] Asked only of those who believed they had insurance coverage.

[e] Asked only of persons submitting claims.

[f] Asked only of persons claiming to have been treated unfairly. Percentages do not add up to 100% because of multiple complaints.

Percentages of Serious Events for which
Insurance Payments Were Received

Fires	76
Tornadoes	61
Hurricanes	56
Floods	22
Earthquakes	8

Clearly, losses from fire and tornado hazards were covered most completely by insurance, and those from floods and earthquake damage were least covered.

By and large, those who filed claims were satisfied with the outcomes, as indicated in Sections D and E. In every hazard type, a majority of those who filed claims were satisfied that they had been treated fairly by the insurance company involved (Section D). As one might expect, satisfaction was greatest in connection with the hazard claims for which the probability of having claims honored was highest: fires, tornadoes, and hurricanes, as contrasted to floods and earthquakes.

The major specific complaint made by those claiming unfair treatment concerned the size of the payment, two-thirds or more of the dissatisfied indicating that the payment was too small. For the hazards for which coverage was slight, complaints were registered that the claims were disallowed. Few claimed that the payments were too slow in coming or that insurance personnel acted impolitely.

In Table 6.2 we consider the amounts paid by insurance companies for damages of various kinds. Note that *all* hazard events with nonzero damages are grouped together in this table, with no distinctions made among serious and minor events. Each of the sections from A to E considers the sources of the damages involved, with the final section, F, considering all damages summed together.

Fire insurance payments were made in more than one-half of the cases of fires (57%), with average payment being close to $10,000. Payments for damages to real property were most fre-

TABLE 6.2
Adjusted Insurance Claims Reimbursed by Hazard Type[a]
(Cases with Damage Amounts Greater Than Zero, N = 884)

Damage type	Fire (N = 218)	Flood (N = 112)	Hurricane (N = 144)	Tornado (N = 365)	Earthquake (N = 44)
A. Damage to buildings					
No payment[a]	57%	94%	62%	64%	96%
Average amount reimbursed[b]	$3,637	$367	$1,022	$693	$88
Average payment[c]	$8,434	$5,865	$2,675	$1,916	$1,935
B. Injuries and illnesses					
No payment[a]	98%	100%	100%	99.5%	100%
Average amount[b]	$5	0	0	$3	0
Average payment[c]	$267	0	0	$624	0
C. Personal property					
No payment[a]	62%	92%	92%	95%	96%
Average amount[b]	$1,857	$157	$184	$158	$30
Average payment[c]	$4,549	$1,958	$2,420	$3,042	$678

(continued)

TABLE 6.2

Adjusted Insurance Claims Reimbursed by Hazard Type[a]

(Cases with Damage Amounts Greater Than Zero, N = 884)

Damage type	Fire (N = 218)	Flood (N = 112)	Hurricane (N = 144)	Tornado (N = 365)	Earthquake (N = 44)
D. Cars and trucks					
No payment[a]	98%	95%	97%	90%	100%
Average amount[b]	$72	$124	$35	$143	0
Average payment[c]	$317	$2,327	$1,011	$1,456	0
E. Other damages					
No payment[a]	95%	95%	83%	86%	98%
Average amount[b]	$248	$27	$129	$292	$60
Average payment[c]	$4,519	$504	$778	$2,138	$2,645
E. Total damages					
No payment[a]	43%	81%	56%	53%	93%
Average amount[b]	$5,820	$675	$1,371	$1,291	$178
Average payment[c]	$10,150	$3,603	$3,085	$2,756	$2,624

[a]Includes cases with missing values on amounts, or types of coverage as zero payment.
[b]Average amount defined as average over all cases, including those with zero payments, adjusted to 1980 dollars.
[c]Average payment defined only over cases receiving nonzero payments and adjusted to 1980 dollars.

quent (43% of the fires),[3] with average payments of more than $8,400. Claims for personal property damage were honored in 38% of the cases, with average payments amounting to almost $4,500. Other categories of payments were received in only a very small minority of cases, in all cases under 5%.

In most of the flood damage cases, no insurance payments were made (81%), and average payments, when received, were about $3,600. The most frequent category of payment was for damages to buildings, with average payments for that purpose being a bit more than $5,800.

Greater insurance coverage was obtained for hurricane and tornado damages, in which payments were received in 44% and 47% of the cases, respectively. Damages to buildings were most often covered.

Earthquakes, as we learned earlier, were the least well covered hazard event, with claims being paid for only about 7% of such events.

As shown in Tables 6.1 and 6.2, the extent to which insurance payments can help a household recover from the ill effects of a hazard event varies by the kind of event experienced and the kinds of damages inflicted. There are additional variations by the characteristics of households, as Table 6.3 shows. An item in the mailed questionnaire asked respondents to estimate the proportion of their total dollar losses that was covered by insurance claim payments.[4] Using these responses as a dependent variable,

---

[3]Note that this proportion is less than that calculated earlier because cases with missing information on amounts paid and on specific categories of coverage were counted in Table 6.2 as zero payments.

[4]The responses were as follows (for those with any damages reported):

No claim payments	49%
1%–9%	2
10%–29%	3
30%–49%	4
50%–69%	7
70%–89%	12
90%–100%	21
100% =	(860)
Don't know and no answer	3%

TABLE 6.3

Regression of Percentage of Loss Reimbursed by Insurance on Hazard Characteristics and Household Characteristics (Serious Events Only: N = 883)

Independent variables	(Dependent variable is respondents' estimates of percentage of reported loss reimbursed through insurance)	
	b	SE
Hazard type[a]		
Fire	41.14***	(6.56)
Flood	−2.016	(6.99)
Hurricane	25.17***	(6.77)
Tornado	30.94***	(6.18)
Hazard characteristics		
Damage to household[b]	11.92***	(1.09)
Community damage seriousness[c]	1.227	(1.43)
Public services disruption[d]	−2.730**	(.884)
Household characteristics		
Age of oldest person	.1309	(.091)
White[e]	15.06***	(3.80)
Household income ($000's)[f]	−15.16	(12.5)
Number of persons	.4109	(.869)
Education (years)	.4311	(.557)
Renter	−16.95***	(3.72)
Intercept	−50.08***	(12.1)
R^2 =	.308***	
N =	(718)	

[a]Dummy variables: Omitted category is "earthquake."
[b]Reported total dollar loss to household coded into five categories: 0 = no damage, 1 = $1–$50, 2 = $51–$100, 3 = $101–$200, 4 = $201–$500, 5 = over $500.
[c]Index measuring reported damage to homes on block and in neighborhood and community (see questionnaire, Item 34).
[d]Number of public services disrupted as a consequence of event (Item 33 on questionnaire).
[e]Dummy variable: Omitted category is "all nonwhite."
[f]Reported household income in the year the event occurred.
*p is .05 or smaller.
**p is .01 or smaller.
***p is .001 or smaller.

Because these replies were respondent estimates, they are not necessarily accurate reflections of what might be computed if exact damages and insurance payments were known from records. Indeed, the percentage estimates may reflect respondent satisfaction as much as actual payments.

Table 6.3 presents a regression in which independent variables include features of the hazard event and household characteristics.

As we have shown, if the hazard event was a fire, a hurricane, or a tornado, the proportion of losses reimbursed through insurance coverage was considerably greater than in floods and earthquakes. The enhancement was greatest in the case of fire hazards, with 41% more of the losses from such events being reimbursed.

The greater the damage, the larger the proportion reimbursed, a finding that reflects the fact that damages to building structures were usually a large part of the losses reported in high-loss events (see Chapter 5). The context of the event had little or no effect on the losses reimbursed. Damages to other buildings on the street or in the neighborhood or the larger community affected the proportion reimbursed little or not at all. Loss reimbursement was affected slightly by the disruption of public services: For each public service that was disrupted, almost 3% less insurance reimbursement was experienced. It is difficult to interpret this finding: Possibly, it reflects the greater likelihood of such interruptions in earthquakes and floods, as compared with the other hazard events.[5]

The main differences among households concerned tenure and race. Renters were not as likely to be reimbursed as much through payments (17% less), and whites were more likely to get a higher proportion of losses reimbursed (by about 15%). These differences are very likely reflections of the differences in insurance coverage: Almost all home owners are required by their mortgagors to have insurance covering real property, whereas many renters carry little or no insurance to cover their personal possessions. The racial differences may also reflect differences in insurance purchases, but this is mainly a speculation.

---

[5]Another possibility: Disruptions of local community services are one explicit reason for a federal disaster declaration. Thus, events that cause a disruption of community services are more likely to be federally declared. In consequence, victims of such events are more likely to be eligible for various federal disaster-relief funds, which would in turn tend to reduce the proportion of total loss for which insurance reimbursements would be made.

OTHER FINANCIAL AID RECEIVED

Although insurance claims are a major source of financial aid to households experiencing hazard losses, there are many other agencies that also provide financial help to victims. In addition, neighbors, friends, and especially relatives may provide gifts and loans. Indeed, for hazard events that are not ordinarily covered by home owners' insurance policies, loans and gifts may be the only financial help available.

Table 6.4 presents tabulations of those who received loans and gifts or grants from all sources (excluding, of course, any insurance claim payments). Loans were received in proportions ranging from 13% in the case of flood hazards down to 5% for tornado events. The amounts obtained (corrected for inflation) tended to be fairly large, especially in the case of fires and floods, for which the average loans were $8,615 and $16,604, respectively, probably for the reconstruction of real property damaged in the event.

Gifts and grants were more frequently received but were usually of a smaller magnitude. Gifts and grants were received by 28% of the households experiencing a flood, with the average grant being slightly over $7,000, but by only 6% of the tornado victims, the average grant in such cases being slightly more than $600.

Grants and loans combined were quite frequent. More than one-third of all the flood households (34%) received some sort of financial help of this sort, with the average amount being over $12,000. In contrast, only 9% of tornado victim households received any financial help, with the average amount being slightly more than $8,000.

The sources providing financial aid are shown in Table 6.5. As might be expected, only small minorities of households receive aid from any one of the sources, the largest percentage in the table (19%) representing the proportion of flood hazard events in which support was received from the American National Red Cross. Most of the proportions in the table are close to zero.

In the case of fires, the most frequent sources of financial help

TABLE 6.4

Loans, Gifts, and Grants Received from All Sources[a]
(Events with Nonzero Damages Only: N = 883)[b]

Type of aid[c]	Fires (N = 218)	Floods (N = 112)	Hurricanes (N = 144)	Tornadoes (N = 365)	Earthquakes (N = 44)	All combined (N = 883)
All loans						
Percentage receiving loan(s)	6	13	7	5	9	8
Average ($)[d]	$553	$2,223	$423	$496	$615	$724
Average loan[e]	$8,615	$16,604	$6,094	$10,665	$6,765	$10,650
All grants and gifts						
Percentage receiving grant(s) or gift(s)	7	28	7	6	14	10
Average	$162	$1,942	$253	$35	$661	$375
Average Grant[e]	$986	$7,015	$3,643	$623	$4,802	$3,189
Combined loans and grants						
Percentages receiving loans and/or grants	20	34	12	9	16	14
Average[d]	$716	$4,165	$676	$532	$1,276	$1,099
Average loan and/or grant[c]	$3,630	$12,277	$5,728	$6,075	$8,024	$7,084

[a] Adjusted to 1980 dollars and outlying values trimmed.
[b] Includes only events with nonzero damages.
[c] Includes loans, gifts, and grants received from all sources indicated in Table 6.5 and excludes insurance payments.
[d] Averaged over all events, including those with no grants or loans.
[e] Average for those receiving grants (or loans).

TABLE 6.5

Financial Aid Received from Various Sources
(Events with Nonzero Damage Only: N = 883)[a]

Source of financial aid	Percentages receiving aid[b]				
	Fires	Floods	Hurricanes	Tornadoes	Earthquakes
Federal agencies					
SBA business loan	0	10	9	0	0
SBA personal loan	0	15	4	1	9
Farmers Home Administration	0.5	1	0	0.7	0
FDAA	0	8	3	0.7	3
FEMA	0	0	3	0.3	0
Veterans' Administration	0	0	0.9	0.3	0
Unemployment payments	0	2	0.9	0.3	0
Other federal agency	1	5	3	0.3	0
American National Red Cross	5	19	0.9	1	3
State and local government					
State agency	2	3	0.9	0	0
Local agency	1	0	0	0	0
Other local sources					
Local bank	4	3	0	3	0
Local community organization	4	1	0	0	0
Church or synagogue	7	3	0.9	1	0
Labor union	1	1	0	0	0
Employer	6	5	3	0.3	0
Relatives	10	15	5	5	9

[a]Includes only events with nonzero dollar damages.
[b]Includes all aid: grants, gifts, and loans.

were local ones, relatives helping out in 1 out of 10 such cases, with the next most frequent source (7%) being local churches and synagogues. Of the national-level agencies, only the Red Cross made a significant (5%) showing as a source of financial aid, mainly in the form of grants and gifts to victims.

The victims of floods were more likely to be helped by almost every source: 15% were helped by relatives, 19% by the Red Cross, and 15% by the Small Business Administration (SBA) personal loan program, with an additional 10% aided by that agency's business loan program. Indeed, the level of overall help given in flood events was high enough to reach one out of three victimized households.

Hurricane events also activated many agencies but not at as high a level as in the case of floods. The Small Business Administration, the Federal Emergency Management Administration (FEMA), and the Federal Disaster Assistance Administration (FDAA) were all sources of financial help used by up to 9% of the victimized families.

Tornado events were responded to by fewer sources and less frequently than other hazards by those who did respond. Only relatives reached as many as 5% of the victimized households, local bank loans being the nearest competitor, with a 3% coverage. The remainder of the sources were all 1% or below.

Finally, earthquakes were even more eclectic in terms of the sources from which financial aid came. The Small Business Administration's personal loan program reached 9% of the victimized households. Relatives responded at about the same level (9%), but the remaining sources were mainly at zero. Of course, there were few (44) earthquake events with nonzero damage in the sample, and hence, these estimates are subject to a considerable amount of small sample fluctuation.

Although it is difficult to discern an overall patterning in the sources of noninsurance financial aid to victims of natural hazards, important roles appear to be played by the federal agencies that have disaster relief as a major mission. In addition, the American National Red Cross is present to a significant degree in almost all serious events. Finally, kinship ties always appear to be important.

If there is an overall pattern, it is that gifts and loans are most important when traditional insurance coverage is absent. The complementary roles played by insurance payments and gifts and loans are perhaps best seen in Table 6.6, in which the total dollar

TABLE 6.6

Regressions of Damages[a] ($) on Insurance Payments, Grants, and Loans by Disaster Types (Nonzero Damage Events Only: $N = 883$) (Dependent Variable Is Damages in Percent Estimated as Result of Hazard Event)

Hazard type	R^2	Insurance payments (percent) b/SE	Grants/ gifts (percent) b/SE	Loans (percent) b/SE	Intercept b/SE	N
A. All hazards combined	.09***	1.363*** (.175)	1.330* (.525)	.7224** (.269)	3,915** (1306)	(883)
B. Fire	.45***	1.281*** (.112)	3.684** (1.51)	.7018* (.323)	5,433*** (1362)	(218)
C. Flood	.01	1.363 (3.51)	.7772 (1.59)	.5874 (1.085)	16,218 (10394)	(112)
D. Hurricane	.83***	1.471*** (.066)	-.3414 (.374)	1.397*** (.206)	998.4* (326)	(144)
E. Tornado	.56***	1.585*** (.097)	4.237* (2.06)	.4655 (.133)	947.5* (467)	(365)
F. Earthquake	.70***	.6904 (.507)	1.060*** (.171)	1.204*** (.178)	1,035* (409)	(44)
G. Fires, hurricanes, and tornadoes combined	.52***	1.419*** (.059)	1.748** (.530)	.5993*** (.124)	2,290*** (467)	(727)

[a]Dollars are unadjusted for inflation.
*p is .05 or less.
**p is .01 or less.
***p is .001 or less.

loss has been regressed on insurance payments received, grants and gifts, and loans, separately for each of the hazard event types and for combinations of hazard events. Note that these regressions are not intended to imply that the dollar losses experienced by households were in some way determined by the claims honored or by the loans and gifts received. Rather, the interpretation of the findings should be in noncausal terms: A coefficient for insurance claims, for example, should be interpreted as the coverage of each dollar of damage loss by each insurance-claim payment dollar. Thus, a coefficient of 2.0 means that a dollar of insurance payment covered $2 of loss, net of the coverage provided by gifts and loans. Correspondingly, the R^2 for each of the equations expresses the extent to which the financial aid given was sensitive to the amount of loss experienced by the households. A high R^2 therefore means that the combined financial aid was sensitive to dollar loss, rising as the loss was great and declining otherwise.

First, it should be noted that the R^2 for the combined hazards (as shown in Section A) is relatively low (.09), indicating that there was no particularly strong patterning of financial aid for all the natural hazards combined. The individual R^2's in the remaining equations, however, are quite diverse, indicating that the patterning was different for each of the disasters. Especially striking is the R^2 of essentially zero for floods, indicating that the financial aid sources were not at all sensitive to the amount of loss experienced by the households in question. Insurance coverage, loans, and gifts appear to have been arbitrarily or capriciously given in flood events, responding perhaps to other factors besides how much damage or loss had been experienced by the households.

The remaining disaster types each present somewhat different patterns. As we have seen previously, insurance payments played an important role in fire hazard events, each dollar of insurance payments covering $1.28 of fire loss ($b = 1.281$), net of gifts and loans. Each dollar of grants and gifts covered about $3.68 of losses, and the role of loans appears not to have been structured at all. All told, the equation accounts for 45% of the variance in dollar damage, indicating some degree of indeterminateness in financial help for fire victimization.

In contrast, the equation for hurricane events is more highly structured ($R^2 = .83$), with insurance payments and loans being strongly related to total damage. Each dollar of insurance payment covered $1.47, and each dollar of loans covered $1.39 of the total damage.

Tornado events also appear to be fairly well structured as well, the equation accounting for 56% of the variation in dollar loss. Here, insurance payments and grants or gifts were the main sources that varied with the amount of damage. In contrast, for earthquake events, slightly more structured than tornadoes ($R^2 = .70$), the main factors appear to have been loans and gifts.

The final Section (G) of Table 6.6 considers the three disasters—fires, hurricanes, and tornadoes—in which insurance coverage plays an important role. In that equation, all three sources of financial help were important, each dollar of insurance payment covering $1.42 of loss; each grant dollar, $1.75; and each loan dollar, $0.60.[6]

Over all events, a little more than half (52%) of the households received some financial aid from one or more sources. As shown in Table 6.7, the proportions receiving any financial aid ranged from two out of three households experiencing fires to about one out of four earthquake-victimized households. The amounts received were not trivial, ranging from $5,653 for the average fire-victimized household to $1,455 for the average earthquake victim. Of course, the average payments (money received by those who received some money) were even higher: $10,112 for

---

[6]A coefficient of less than 1.00 suggests that the source in question provided more financial aid than the dollar losses would appear to warrant. However, this particular interpretation is not warranted when other sources of aid were considerably above 1.00. Indeed, in the case of the last equation in Table 6.6, the coefficient for loans (.5993) simply means that loans were more sensitive to the total amount of damages, net of the contribution of other sources. Thus, loans were used to cover more of the losses than gifts or insurance payments.

TABLE 6.7

Total[a] Financial Aid Received and Amounts of Uncovered Losses by Hazard (Only Households with Nonzero Losses = 883)

	Fire (218)	Flood (112)	Hurricane (144)	Tornado (365)	Earthquake (44)	All combined (883)
A. Total aid received						
Percentage receiving some aid	67	46	49	51	23	50
Average aid received	$5,653	$ 4,695	$2,034	$1,524	$1,455	$3,026
Average amount received	$8,383	$10,112	$4,186	$3,008	$6,404	$5,758
B. Financial gap (total loss minus all financial aid[b])						
Average gap	$5,403	$ 5,618	$1,473	$ 940	$1,145	$2,732
C. Increased liabilities (uncovered losses + loans)						
Average increased liabilities	$6,711	$ 8,105	$1,897	$1,601	$1,760	$3,749
D. Increased debt burden (loans as proportion of annual household income[a])						
Percentage	7.3	17.2	3.1	8.6	6.9	8.5

[a]All dollar amounts adjusted to 1980 dollars. Outlying values have been trimmed.
[b]"All financial aid" includes insurance payments, loans, gifts, and grants.

flood victims and $3,008 for tornado victims, with the average payment overall being $5,758.[7]

The financial aid received typically did not cover the full amount of the losses incurred. On average, financial aid fell some $2,732 short of covering the total losses inflicted. For many households, such amounts were nontrivial. The gap between financial aid and total losses was especially high for fires and floods, being around $5,500 for those events.

Disaster events can be regarded as increasing a family's liabilities, some of which are alleviated by grants and gifts. Although loans may help to restore a household to normal functioning, a loan represents a financial obligation that has to be repaid along with interest charges. The sum of uncovered losses plus loans can be regarded as a household's increased financial liabilities, as in Section C of Table 6.7. On the average, households incurred almost $4,000 in increased liabilities, with fires and floods inflicting liabilities of close to $7,000 and $8,000, respectively. In short, the average fire or flood event saddled a household with liabilities that amounted to the cost of a medium-sized car, or about one-fourth to one-third of annual household income.

Section D looks at financial liabilities in still another way. In that section, the amounts of loans received are expressed as percentages of current annual household income.[8] This measure of increased debt burden amounted to 8.5%, varying from a high of 17.2% for flood victims to a low of 3.1% for hurricane victims. Although these proportions do not appear to be very high, they do not take into account carrying charges or existing debts. Hence, the actual impact of the increased debt burden occasioned by hazard victimization may be considerable. A household that dedi-

---

[7]In conjunction with the findings of Table 6.4, it becomes clear that insurance payments played an extremely important role, with two out of every three dollars received coming to the households in the form of insurance payments. Of course, for those risks not normally covered by insurance, financial aid was largely in the form of loans.

[8]Household income was measured as of the year in which the event occurred.

cated 30% of its income to paying off a home mortgage may find an additional 10% needed to pay off a home repair loan a severe burden that eats into income budgeted for education, food, or other necessities. Especially onerous appear to be the debt burdens imposed by flood events.

Table 6.8 looks at how the financial burdens, unrelieved by insurance payments and gifts, were distributed among households and among disaster types. The first column contains the results of regressing the gap between the total loss incurred and the monies received from insurance payments, gifts, and loans on household and hazard event characteristics. Presumably, these are the sums that the households would have had to raise out of their current income or savings to replace or repair damaged property. Of the household characteristics, only race seems to count: Whites had about $2,400 less of a financial gap than nonwhites and Hispanics. The more widespread the disaster, the less the gap, possibly because of the grant and loan programs that were triggered by the size of the hazard event. But the more public services were disrupted, the bigger the gap, an outcome that is not easily explained.

The second column of Table 6.8 is concerned with increased liabilities (uncovered losses plus loans). Increased liabilities were smaller for renters, whites, and more affluent families. Liabilities increased with the number of public services that were disrupted, and fire and flood events left households with greater financial liabilities than other hazard events.

The third column concerns debt burden, the proportion of household income that loans constituted. Virtually nothing predicted debt burden, except disruptions of public services, a marginally significant finding indicating that burdens increased the more public services were disrupted.

None of the regressions shown in Table 6.8 account for much of the variances involved. By and large, it appears that financial liabilities resulting from hazard events impact more strongly on nonwhites and Hispanics and are more likely to arise out of severe fires and floods, but no other strong findings appear.

TABLE 6.8
Regressions of Gap Measures[a] on Household and Disaster
Characteristics (N = 712)

Independent variables	Total loss—financial aid	Increase in liabilities	Debt burden
	b/SE	b/SE	b/SE
Household characteristics			
Household size	70.21	227.0	.0148
	(209)	(201)	(.019)
Education (years)	−173.6	−165.7	−.0154
	(134)	(129)	(.012)
Renter	−637.1	−1,859*	−.0453
	(891)	(857)	(.083)
White	−2,370**	−2,209*	−.9425
	(913)	(878)	(.086)
Age of oldest person	−18.05	−27.59	−.0022
(years)	(22.0)	(24.2)	(.002)
Household income	1.494	−41.56*	Not
($000) at time of event	(22.2)	(21.3)	Applicable
Hazard event characteristics			
1975 or later	945.7	−132.1	−.0046
	(715)	(638)	(.067)
Context seriousness	−813.9*	−323.4	.0418
	(343)	(330)	(.032)
Public service disruptions	1,554***	2,244***	.0475*
	(212)	(204)	(.020)
Hazard types			
Flood	3,069	3,451*	−.0061
	(1,693)	(1,621)	(.159)
Hurricane	−777.1	−208.3	−.1445
	(1,665)	(1,602)	(.568)
Fire	3,904*	5,149**	.0469
	(1,589)	(1,465)	(.149)
Tornado	−185.5	−581.4	−.0278
	(1,523)	(1,465)	(.143)
Intercept	4,605***	5,676*	.2670
	(273)	(2,631)	(.258)
R^2 =	.139***	.253***	.025

[a]All dollars adjusted to 1980 dollars. Outliers are trimmed.
[b]See Table 6.7 for definition of dependent variables.
  *p is less than .05.
 **p is less than .01.
***p is less than .001.

EQUITY IN FINANCIAL HELP

Because the three kinds of financial help so far considered tend to complement one another, depending mainly on the patterns of insurance coverage associated with the different hazard types, it makes some sense to consider who gets any financial help from all of the three sources considered together. Table 6.9 shows the percentages receiving any help from any source, separately for each of the disaster types. In that table, we consider serious events separately from the minor ones, a factor that sharply conditions whether a household received any financial help.

Only small minorities of the households experiencing minor losses received any financial help. In 7% of minor household fires, some financial help was received, but none of the minor flood, hurricane, or earthquake households received any help at all. In addition, 2% of minor tornado events were accompanied by some financial help. Given the results of the previous sections, it was primarily insurance payments that were involved in the minor hazard events.

Proportions ranging between 77% (serious fires) and 17% (earthquakes) of the households experiencing major hazard events received some financial help. Note that, in each case, help was

TABLE 6.9
Percentages Receiving Any Financial Help[a] by Hazard Type and Hazard Event Seriousness

Hazard seriousness[b]	Fires	Floods	Hurricanes	Tornadoes	Earthquakes
Serious	77	48	55	57	17
N =	(223)	(152)	(144)	(316)	(59)
Minor	7	0	0	2	0
N =	(45)	(27)	(117)	(225)	(304)

[a]"Any financial help" means insurance payments, and/or gifts, and/or loans from any of the sources considered in Tables 6.1–6.5.
[b]A serious hazard event was one in which the household claimed damages of $50 or more. A minor event was one in which reported damages were under $50.

TABLE 6.10

Regressions of Any Financial Help on Household Characteristics (All Households Included: N = 1,296)[a] (Dependent Variable Is Receiving Any Financial Help from Insurance, Grants, and/or Loans)

Independent variables	Fires b/SE	Floods b/SE	Hurricanes b/SE	Tornadoes b/SE	Earthquakes b/SE	All hazards combined b/SE
Household characteristics						
Age of oldest person in house	.0039* (.002)	-.0035 (.002)	.0007 (.015)	-.0004 (.001)	.0001 (.001)	.0004 (.001)
Household income (00's)[b]	-.0491** (.020)	-.0927* (.045)	-.0387 (.036)	-.0347* (.015)	-.0114 (.010)	-.0372*** (.010)
White	-.1005 (.064)	.1906 (.103)	-.0893 (.057)	.1005* (.052)	.0085 (.020)	.0676** (.025)
Renter	-.2260** (.062)	-.1331 (.088)	-.0551 (.057)	-.0758 (.048)	.0090 (.018)	-.0884*** (.024)
Education (years)	.0040 (.011)	-.0034 (.016)	.0076 (.010)	-.0081 (.007)	-.0018 (.003)	-.0047 (.004)
Household size	-.0729 (.0167)	.0246 (.025)	.0051 (.014)	-.0042 (.011)	.0046 (.005)	-.0018 (.006)
Hazard characteristics						
Community seriousness[c]	-.0591 (.071)	.0632 (.041)	.0103 (.022)	.0182 (.018)	.0279 (.019)	-.0197 (.011)
Public service interruptions[d]	.0146 (.019)	.0590** (.021)	.0060 (.017)	-.0271* (.014)	.0567*** (.011)	.0091 (.007)

Property damage[e]	.1493*** (.014)	.0742*** (.020)	.1597*** (.013)	.1456*** (.009)	.0433*** (.007)	.1305*** (.053)
Hazard type[f]						
Fire			Not Applicable			.1587*** (.035)
Flood			Not Applicable			−.1119** (.039)
Hurricane			Not Applicable			.0008 (.032)
Tornado			Not Applicable			.0099 (.027)
Intercept	.0632 (.197)	.0239 (.250)	−.1952 (.167)	.1269 (.128)	.0096 (.058)	.0607 (.051)
R^2 =	.48	.44	.64	.46	.44	.53
N =	(208)	(116)	(196)	(473)	(282)	(1,296)

[a]All households, whether or not they experienced any damages, are included in these equations. Missing values on any of the independent variables account for N's being smaller than those reported in Table 5.1.

[b]Household income was measured as of the year of the hazard event.

[c]An index consisting of whether damages were sustained by other households on the same block in the same neighborood and in the same community.

[d]Consists of a count of the number of public services interrupted as a consequence of the hazard event.

[e]Measured in categories (see Table 6.2 for codes used), unadjusted for inflation.

[f]Dummy variables: Omitted category is "earthquakes."

    *p is .05 or less.

  **p is .01 or less.

 ***p is .001 or less.

made up of different combinations of insurance payments, gifts, and loans.

The issue of who got any financial help is addressed in Table 6.10. A dummy variable that takes on the value of 1 if a household received any financial help and 0 if the household received none at all is the dependent variable in each of the regression equations of that table. The coefficients are therefore interpretable in terms of changes in the probability of receiving any financial help. Thus, a coefficient of −.2260 for renters indicates that renters, net of any other characteristics, were about .23 less likely to receive any financial help compared with owners.

The R^2 for each of the equations represents the extent to which the characteristics shown in the equations determined the probability of receiving any financial help. It should be noted that these coefficients are fairly large, the smallest being .44 and the largest .64, indicating that the independent variables accounted for between 44% and 64% of the variation among households in the probability of receiving any financial help.

A consistent finding in each of the equations concerns the effects of the amount of damage on the probability of receiving financial help of some sort. For each of the disaster types, the greater the damage amount, the more likely the household was to receive some aid. The probability differences for damage range from .16 for hurricanes to .04 for earthquakes, but in every case, they are statistically significant.[9]

For the remaining factors considered in Table 6.10, no consistent pattern can be detected across hazard types. With regard to fires, the higher a family's income, the less the probability of receiving financial help—possibly because the available financial resources of more affluent families allowed them to avoid the necessity of asking for loans or receiving gifts. Renters, compared

[9]The total amount of damage is coded into five categories, each encompassing a different range in dollars. The coefficients indicate shifts in probability associated with a shift from one of the coded categories to another, an amount that may be as little as $50 in the first category and many thousands of dollars in the last (and highest) category. See Table 6.2 for a description of the coded categories.

with owners, had a much lower probability of receiving any financial help, at least partially because fewer renters carried fire insurance coverage on their personal possessions. No other factor appears to have been significant for fire hazards.

Flood hazards occurring to higher income families were also less likely to be accompanied by financial help. Flood events that involved the interruption of public utilities and services were also more likely to be met with financial assistance. Because such interruptions are more likely to occur with widespread flooding, this finding suggests that the relief activities of the federal government and such national organizations as the Red Cross are more likely to be triggered when the event involves larger areas. None of the other factors had significant coefficients.

Nothing besides amount of damage determined whether financial help was obtained in the case of hurricane events. Apparently, insurance coverage was universal enough for this hazard event to produce rough equity among households.

Financial aid in the case of tornado events also appears to have been related to income, with the more affluent households less likely to receive any financial help. (Incidentally, receiving financial help is not an unmitigated blessing, because loans may add to the financial burdens of a household, as we saw elsewhere in this chapter.) Tornado events that were accompanied by the disruption of public services and utilities were less likely to be met with financial help, a pattern that appears to be counterintuitive and hence resists reasonable interpretation.

Earthquake assistance was affected only by the interruption of public services: The more such interruptions, the more likely outside financial aid was to be rendered.

Finally, in the last column of Table 6.10, all hazard types have been combined. Across all types, higher income families were less likely to receive (or solicit) financial aid, renters were less likely than owners to receive such help, and whites were more likely to be financial aid recipients. But the most important patterns in the last column are the effects of disaster types. Fires were much more likely to be accompanied by financial aid, and floods were less likely (as compared with earthquakes). Neither hurricanes nor tornadoes were distinguishable statistically from earthquakes.

Overall, the patterning of financial aid does not spell out a serious degree of inequity through the lack of access to financial help. The major pattern that emerges is that the probability of financial help rises with the amount of damage experienced. We have a bit of a hint that such help is not always an unmitigated blessing, because the more affluent families appeared to be less likely to receive financial aid (or to ask for it). Perhaps the major bias is against renting families, possibly through the more usual lack of insurance coverage among that group.

It should be noted that the data presented in this section do not contradict those of the previous section. The size of the gap between financial aid and the losses experienced apparently was not affected by the same factors as whether one received any financial aid. The gap was influenced mainly by the size of the losses incurred, whereas the probability of receiving aid was influenced by losses and other factors having to do with the insurability of the hazard risk and the kinds of government programs available, factors that in turn were influenced by the type of hazard involved and the geographical extent of the hazard.

Informal Sources of Help

Although financial help is certainly important, especially in the cases in which critical household resources have been damaged or destroyed, other types of help may also be of considerable use and indeed may substitute for financial help in some cases. A family may have need of temporary shelter, and an offer of a place to live for a short period may be crucial to the comfort of a household in the immediate aftermath of any of the hazard events under study. Or some donated labor may be even more useful than funds, if, for example, all that is needed to restore some degree of livability to a home is the removal of the debris left by the event or, perhaps, the clearing of a driveway.

As previous studies of the immediate aftermath of natural hazard events have shown, a great deal of help is provided to victimized households by neighbors, friends, relatives, co-workers, local churches, and employers. Indeed, as Table 6.11 shows, large proportions of the households in the study reported some help from one or more of these sources. Especially in serious events, more than a third of the families reported receiving help from friends, relatives, and neighbors. Smaller proportions received help from churches, employers, and co-workers, but these proportions in no case were less than 5% (employers). Households experiencing minor hazard events reported correspondingly less help from such sources, in all cases less than 6%.

The forms of help emphasized services or goods in kind. In a majority of cases, labor services were the main form of aid rendered. More than four out of five (84%) of the instances of neighbors' giving help consisted of labor. Another large category of aid was the offer of shelter. About two out of five (38%) cases of help from relatives involved shelter. Much less frequent were loans and gifts, some in the form of money and others in the form of goods or services.

As can be seen in Section G, on the average, households experiencing serious hazard events received help from slightly more than one source (1.24), whereas those in minor events received help from .28 sources, on the average. In short, when in need, some form of help is available: Whether that help is sufficient, however, is another story.

Many of the organizations that provide financial help also provide other kinds of aid. For example, on the sites of major disasters, federal agencies often set up disaster aid stations that provide information to victims about many of the problems that face them, from advice on how to file insurance claims to places where one can obtain emergency food supplies. Voluntary organizations, such as the Red Cross or the Mennonite Relief Organiza-

TABLE 6.11
Forms of Aid from Informal Sources by Hazard Type and Seriousness

Source of aid	Proportions giving aid						Types of aid given[a]				
	Fire	Flood	Hurricane	Tornado	Earthquake	Combined	Shelter (%)	Loans (%)	Gifts (%)	Labor (%)	N^b
A. Friends (percent)											
Serious	36	46	41	32	14	35	21	2	18	78	(315)
Minor	9	11	4	5	c	3					
B. Relatives (percent)											
Serious	41	56	30	32	16	36	38	9	21	66	(342)
Minor	12	33	8	7	1	6					
C. Neighbors (percent)											
Serious	30	32	38	28	10	30	10	1	18	84	(265)
Minor	5	11	4	6	0	3					

D. Church or synagogue (percent)										
Serious	13	11	3	4	2	7	8	2	73	35	(60)
Minor	0	0	0	1	0	c					
E. Co-workers (percent)										
Serious	10	11	8	6	4	8	4	1	37	66	(73)
Minor	0	0	0	1	c	1					
F. Employers (percent)										
Serious	5	9	7	4	0	5	10	13	55	35	(40)
Minor	2	0	0	c	0	c					
G. Help from all sources										
Serious	1.34	1.57	1.26	1.02	.39	1.23					
Minor	.27	.56	.15	.20	.01	.28					
Approximate N for above[d]										
Serious	(222)	(119)	(142)	(342)	(50)	(875)					
Minor	(43)	(27)	(111)	(206)	(285)	(687)					

[a]All hazard events combined in these tabulations.

[b]N shown is number of families receiving some aid from the source in question.

[c]Less than .5% but larger than zero.

[d]N's shown are for the classes directly above each entry. Actual N's vary by one or two cases, depending on missing data.

tion, also set up on-site, providing a wide spectrum of help and aid. The extent of such contact between agencies and victims is shown in Table 6.12.

Contacts with the FDAA were claimed by 4% of the households in all serious hazard events, with another 1% claiming contacts with the FEMA. Note that none of the families that were involved in minor hazard events claimed contacts with either federal agency. As one can expect from the earlier parts of this chapter, contacts with the FDAA and the FEMA were especially prevalent for serious flood events and were virtually nonexistent for fires.

About the same level of contact frequency was claimed with the Small Business Administration, about 5%—distributed in much the same way as contacts with the FEMA and the FDAA. About one in four of the serious flood households had some contact with the SBA and virtually none who were in serious fires. Contact with the Farmers Home Administration, the Veterans Administration, and units of regular army were relatively rare, each showing contact with about 1% of the households in serious hazard events.

The American National Red Cross apparently earns its high reputation for responsiveness to natural hazard events; in our study, it registered high levels of contact in connection with each type of event. Indeed, one in four of the households experiencing a serious flood event claimed that it was contacted by the Red Cross. The lowest level of contact (4%) was registered in connection with earthquakes. The Salvation Army registered about half the level of contact of the Red Cross, but enough to show for every type of hazard event, except earthquakes. Finally, the Mennonite Relief Organization contacted about half the proportions that claimed contact with the Salvation Army relief workers. These three private relief organizations were especially likely to be present during floods and hurricanes and together represented as much presence on the site as all of the federal government agencies considered together. This is not to say that their roles in providing relief were as important or more important, because the

TABLE 6.12
Contacts with Relief and Rescue Organizations by Hazard Type and Seriousness of Event

Organization		Percentage contacted by						Percentage highly satisfied $N = a$	Percentage helped by organization $N = a$
		Fire	Flood	Hurricane	Tornado	Earthquake	All hazards		
A. Federal agencies									
FDAA	Serious	b	11	7	2	2	4	55 (29)	50 (30)
	Minor	0	0	0	0	0	0	—	—
SBA	Serious	b	23	5	2	8	5	55 (38)	81 (41)
	Minor	0	0	0	0	0	0	—	—
Farmers Home Admin.	Serious	1	1	2	1	0	1	29 (7)	75 (9)
	Minor	0	0	0	0	0	0	—	—
FEMA	Serious	0	1	5	1	0	1	78 (9)	100 (9)
	Minor	0	0	0	0	0	0	—	—
Veterans Admin.	Serious	b	2	2	b	0	1	60 (5)	60 (5)
	Minor	0	0	0	0	0	0	—	—
Regular army	Serious	0	0	4	b	0	1	60 (5)	67 (6)
	Minor	0	0	1	1	0	b	33 (3)	33 (3)
B. Private national organizations									
Red Cross	Serious	7	25	8	5	4	8	67 (67)	76 (67)
	Minor	0	0	1	1	0	b	100 (3)	33 (3)
Salvation Army	Serious	2	14	6	2	0	4	77 (30)	72 (30)
	Minor	0	0	0	0	0	0	—	—
Mennonite Relief	Serious	0	5	2	2	0	2	92 (13)	50 (16)
	Minor	0	0	0	b	0	b	—	—

(continued)

TABLE 6.12 (Continued)

Organization		Percentage contacted by						Percentage highly satisfied $N = $ [a]		Percentage helped by organization $N = $ [a]	
		Fire	Flood	Hurricane	Tornado	Earthquake	All hazards				
C. State and local government agencies											
Civil defense	Serious	0	9	5	4	0	4	71	(28)	67	(27)
	Minor	0	0	4	b	0	1	33	(6)	17	(6)
Fire dept.	Serious	48	25	7	5	6	19	76	(151)	77	(146)
	Minor	23	4	4	3	b	3	71	(21)	57	(21)
Police and sheriff	Serious	12	16	10	10	10	11	60	(83)	45	(80)
	Minor	8	0	2	3	1	2	54	(13)	25	(12)
National Guard	Serious	1	13	5	3	2	4	73	(30)	71	(31)
	Minor	0	0	1	b	0	b	50	(2)	0	(2)
Welfare dept.	Serious	5	6	4	1	0	3	39	(63)	91	(22)
	Minor	0	0	0	b	0	b	—		—	

Public works dept. Serious	1	13	7	9	8	7	51 (57)	77 (57)
Public works dept. Minor	0	0	3	2	[b]	1	62 (8)	67 (9)
D. Local private organizations								
Local hospital[c] Serious	3	3	2	2	2	2	82 (17)	79 (19)
Local hospital[c] Minor	0	0	0	[b]	0	[b]	— (—)	— (—)
Labor union Serious	[b]	2	2	[b]	0	1	100 (5)	100 (5)
Labor union Minor	0	0	0	0	0	0	— (—)	— (—)
Civic org. Serious	2	0	1	[b]	0	[b]	80 (10)	73 (11)
Civic org. Minor	0	0	1	[b]	0	[b]	— (—)	— (—)
Local church Serious	9	14	4	6	2	7	80 (54)	79 (53)
Local church Minor	0	0	4	2	0	1	75 (8)	0 (9)
Approx. N's Serious	(213)	(109)	(136)	(333)	(52)	(843)		
Approx. N's Minor	(40)	(27)	(116)	(216)	(286)	(685)		

[a] Based only on persons who had been contacted by the agency in question.

[b] Nonzero but less than 0.5%.

[c] Local hospitals are often run by municipalities and states and hence are not always private, as their classification here suggests.

services rendered were not the same as those provided by the federal agencies. Indeed, as we saw in the last section, the financial aid represented by federal grants and loans was not at all duplicated by the private relief organizations.

As might be expected, state and, especially, local government agencies were important presences on the site during and after hazard events. Especially important were local fire and police departments, contacts with whom were registered by 19% and 11%, respectively, of all the respondents experiencing serious hazard events. Obviously, the highest contact rate of all the agencies considered in Table 6.12 (48%) was registered for fire department contacts in connection with serious fires. If anything, one may question why this frequency of contact with fire departments was not considerably higher, say, at the level of 80%–95%! Fire departments were a frequent presence in all hazard events, contacting one in four of the families experiencing serious flood events, and proportions ranging from 5% to 7% in hurricanes, tornadoes, and earthquakes.

The police were present almost equally and were frequently involved in each of the hazard types. Contact levels of 16% were claimed by flood victims, at one extreme, and by 10% of the earthquake victims at the other. Together, fire and police clearly represented the first line of local community response to hazard events.

The remainder of state and local government agencies were comparatively infrequent sources of contact. Civil defense was less frequently present (4%) than public works departments (7%). The National Guard (4%) was more frequently acknowledged as a point of contact than the local welfare department (3%).

Finally, Table 6.12 considers local private organizations, all of which had low levels of contact, with the exception of local churches and synagogues, which registered 7% contacts with victimized households in serious events. Especially surprising was the low level of contact with local hospitals (2%).[10]

---

[10]We have classified hospitals as private organizations, although it is likely that in many communities such hospitals are at least partially, if not entirely, incorporated into local, county, or state government.

The last two columns of Table 6.12 show the proportions of persons experiencing contacts with the agencies in question who reported themselves to be highly satisfied and the proportions who received "help" from such agencies. Note that the respondents were offered a choice among "high," "medium," and "low" as ways of expressing their degree of satisfaction. The proportions shown in Table 6.12 therefore represent the highest level permitted in the questionnaire. By and large, the majority of persons experiencing contact registered the highest degree of satisfaction with the agency in question. Especially high levels of satisfaction were registered for contacts with national private relief organizations and local agencies, especially where the numbers of contacts were large enough to produce stable percentages.

Levels of satisfaction with federal agencies were not as high, being 55% for both the FDAA and the SBA (where the numbers of households having contacts with those agencies were high enough to warrant paying attention to the results).

In sum, clear pluralities, upward of two in three, were highly satisfied with their contacts with the national relief organizations and local agencies. About one in two registered the same high degree of satisfaction with federal agencies. In no case were there large proportions who claimed to have a low level of satisfaction with their contacts with any of the agencies.

The proportions who received any "help" as a consequence of their contacts with each of the agencies are shown in the last column of Table 6.12. Majorities in almost every case claimed to have received help, the notable exception being contacts with the police departments.

Despite the low levels of contact with any one of the agencies shown in Table 6.12, the cumulative effect of all the agencies taken together was to ensure that the majority of households experiencing serious hazard events were contacted by one or another agency. As shown in Table 6.13, where contacts are cumulated, the average number of contacts received by a household experiencing a serious hazard event was .85 (see Section D of Table 6.13). Indeed, for serious flood hazards, the average rose to 1.81,

TABLE 6.13

Summary of Contacts with Federal Agencies, National Relief
Organizations, and Local Agencies[a]

Average number of contacts with	Number of contacts (average)					
	Fire	Flood	Hurricane	Tornado	Earthquake	Combined
All federal agencies						
Serious	.02	.38	.24	.07	.10	.13
Minor	.00	.00	.00	.01	.00	.01
All local or state agencies (private and government)						
Serious	.81	1.00	.46	.41	.29	.59
Minor	.30	.04	.19	.12	.01	.09
All national relief organizations						
Serious	.08	.43	.16	.08	.04	.14
Minor	.00	.00	.01	.01	.00	.01
All agencies combined						
Serious	.92	1.81	.87	.56	.42	.85
Minor	.30	.04	.21	.14	.01	.10

[a]See Table 6.12 for the specific agencies in each of the classifications used. Approximate N's for Table 6.12 also apply to this table.

indicating that the typical flood victim household was approached by close to two agencies.

Local and state public and private agencies (see Section B) were most active in contacting victimized households, generating an average of .59 contacts in serious events. National relief organizations and federal agencies had about the same average number of contacts, .14 and .13, respectively.

In looking across hazard events, it is clear that the victims of serious flood events are given the most attention by all agencies. Local and state agencies give almost as much attention to serious fires, representing the fact that most such events are regarded as

Table 6.14

Regression of Contacts with Agencies on Hazard and Household
Characteristics: All Mail Survey Households (N = 1,268) (Dependent
Variables Are Counts of Contacts with the Agencies Designated)

Independent variables	Federal agencies b/SE	Local agencies b/SE	Private agencies b/SE	All agencies combined b/SE
Disaster type[a]				
Fire	−.0936***	.4739***	−.0106	.3703**
	(.039)	(.091)	(.035)	(.136)
Flood	.0984*	.1941*	.1534***	.4467**
	(.043)	(.102)	(.049)	(.152)
Hurricane	−.0117	−.1016	−.0404	−.1537
	(.035)	(.082)	(.032)	(.122)
Tornado	−.0810**	−.0501	−.0433	−.1745
	(.029)	(.069)	(.027)	(.103)
Disaster characteristics				
Damage to household[b]	.0120	.0330*	.0092	.0538*
	(.007)	(.016)	(.006)	(.023)
Percentage damage re-imbursed through in-surance[c]	.0004	−.0003	.0001	.0002
	(.001)	(.000)	(.000)	(.001)
Disaster community se-riousness[d]	.0234*	.0660*	.0173	.1069*
	(.019)	(.008)	(.007)	(.028)
Public service disrup-tion[e]	.0549***	.1925***	.0658***	.3134***
	(.008)	(.019)	(.007)	(.028)
Household characteristics				
Age of oldest person[f]	.0011	−.0008	.0005	.0008
	(.001)	(.002)	(.001)	(.002)
Number of persons	.0123	.0277	.0084	.0481*
	(.007)	(.015)	(.006)	(.023)
Renter	−.0182	.0166	.0145	.0131
	(.026)	(.061)	(.024)	(.092)
Household income ($000's)[f]	−.0250**	−.0334	−.0167	−.0750*
	(.009)	(.022)	(.009)	(.030)
Education (years)	−.0034	.0020	−.0042	−.0057
	(.004)	(.010)	(.004)	(.015)
Intercept	.0294	−.0410	.0485	.0386
	(.078)	(.183)	(.072)	(.276)
R^2 =	.21	.14	.17	.23

[a]Dummy variables: Omitted hazard is "earthquake."
[b]Damage coded into five categories. See Table 6.2 for definitions.
[c]Respondent estimate of extent of loss covered by insurance claim payments.
[d]Rating of damages to other homes on block and in neighborhood and community.
[e]Number of public services and utilities interrupted as consequence of event.
[f]Measured as of the year of the event.
*p is .05 or smaller.
**p is .01 or smaller.
***p is .001 or smaller.

local matters. Serious hurricane events receive the next most frequent amount of attention, with tornadoes and earthquakes trailing behind in attention.

Table 6.14 provides another way to summarize the findings of this section. The amount of contact with each of the groupings of agencies shown in Table 6.13 is considered a dependent variable in Table 6.14, with the characteristics of hazard events and households as independent variables. These regression analyses provide some clues to whether contacts with agencies are being distributed equitably among households.

The findings can be easily summarized. First of all, the characteristics of households played almost no role in the number of contacts with any of the agency groupings. Indeed, if anything, there appears to have been a slight bias against the more affluent, the number of contacts overall and with federal agencies declining slightly as income increased. Otherwise, whites as compared with nonwhites, renters compared with owners, large households compared with smaller households, and older households compared with younger ones were all about equally likely to be contacted by federal, local, and relief agencies.

The main determinants of the numbers of contacts were the characteristics of the hazard event and the type of hazard involved. All agencies were more likely to make contacts when the hazard event produced widespread damage and when public services and utilities were disrupted.

Federal agencies were more likely to make contacts during flood hazards but less likely to be available for fires and tornadoes. Local agencies were more available for fires and floods, and private relief organizations were especially available for floods. (All these findings are in comparison with earthquake events.)

HELP FROM ALL SOURCES

The separate sources of help and assistance reviewed so far in this chapter do not necessarily compete with one another. As we have seen, some sources are complementary, and others specialize to some degree, especially the somewhat separate spheres of local and national agencies. Indeed, although any one source may reach a very small minority of affected households, the combined coverage of all sources of aid may be quite large.

In Table 6.15, we present two measures of combined coverage. The first measure (Section A) is based on all the sources of help and contact with the exception of insurance; a household was counted as having received help if it acknowledged contact with any of the agencies discussed in the last section or if it received loans, gifts, or help from informal sources. The coverage of this measure was 63% for all serious hazard events and 13% for the minor events, with an overall coverage of 40%. Help coverage ranged considerably from one hazard type to another: 85% of the

TABLE 6.15
Total Help Received from All Sources

	Fire	Flood	Hurricane	Tornado	Earthquake	Combined hazards
Percentage receiving help from at least one source[a]						
Serious	72	85	65	55	30	63
Minor	33	46	20	16	2	13
Percentage receiving help from at least one source and/or insurance payment[b]						
Serious	94	89	79	77	36	80
Minor	36	46	20	17	2	13
N's for above:						
Serious	(184)	(102)	(126)	(302)	(50)	(764)
Minor	(39)	(26)	(113)	(215)	(284)	(677)

[a]Receiving help from agencies in the form of loans or gifts, or help from informal sources of contact with federal, local, or relief agencies. Counted as 1 if help received from any source; 0 if otherwise.
[b]Same as above, with insurance payment added.

serious flood victimized households received some help from some source, but only 2% of the minor earthquake events involved help.

The bottom section of Table 6.15 presents a measure of help that counts insurance payments as an additional source of help. This more inclusive measure produces a markedly higher coverage: 80% of the serious hazard events were reached either by insurance payments or by some form of help, with 13% of the minor events so covered. The overall coverage percentage was 49%. In short, most (four out of five) of the serious hazard events (damages of $50 or more) were reached by some form of help, with only small minorities of households that suffered serious fire or flood events not being reached by one or another source.

The only hazard event that was not well covered was earthquakes. This finding may simply reflect that the historical period under study contained only one earthquake experience that involved a lot of concentrated damage—the San Fernando quake of 1971—and that most of the earthquake experiences were generated by less serious events.

The two coverage measures of Table 6.15 are considered again in Table 6.16, this time as dependent variables in regression equations. Note that the two equations account for a relatively large amount of variation in help coverage—41% and 56%, respectively—indicating that the independent variables account for a great deal of the variation in receiving help.

This analysis shows rather clearly that the major determinants of receiving help are the type of hazard event experienced and the seriousness of the event for the community or the household. Earthquake victims (the omitted category in the analysis) were, as seen elsewhere, less likely to receive assistance than victims of other hazard types. The more loss a household experienced, and the more widespread the damage throughout the community, the more likely that help would be given. Clearly, the relief agencies and local sources were very sensitive to the need represented by the household's condition and the scope of the hazard event.

TABLE 6.16

Regressions of Any Help and Any Help Plus Insurance Payments on
Hazard and Household Characteristics (N = 1,192)

Independent variables	Any help[a]		Any help or insurance[b]	
	b	SE	b	SE
Hazard type[c]				
Fire	.3531***	(.043)	.3927***	(.037)
Hurricane	.1480***	(.039)	.1702***	(.034)
Flood	.3204***	(.048)	.2639***	(.042)
Tornado	.1180***	(.033)	.1684***	(.028)
Hazard characteristics				
Damage to household[d]	.0622***	(.007)	.1068***	(.006)
Hazard community serious-ness[e]	.0389***	(.014)	.0485***	(.012)
Public service interruptions[f]	.0765***	(.009)	.0397***	(.008)
Percentage loss reimbursed by insurance	−.0001	(.0004)	(Not applicable)	
Household characteristics				
Age of oldest person[g]	−.0026**	(.001)	−.0019**	(.007)
Household income[g]	−.0028**	(.001)	−.0024**	(.000)
Number of persons	−.0024	(.007)	−.0007	(.006)
Renter	−.0201	(.029)	−.0377	(.025)
White	−.0086	(.030)	.0239	(.0265)
Education (years)	−.0002	(.005)	.0006	(.004)
Intercept	.1466	(.087)	.0850	(.076)
R^2 =	.41		.56	

[a]Dummy variable: Coded 1 if respondent received help from any source or had contact with any agency (except insurance payments).
[b]Dummy variables coded 1 if respondent received help from any source, including insurance payments, or had contact with any agency.
[c]Dummy variables: Omitted category is "earthquakes."
[d]Damage amounts coded into intervals. See Table 6.2 for intervals.
[e]Measure of community seriousness consisting of damages to homes on block, or in neighborhood or community.
[f]Number of interruptions to public services and utilities.
[g]Measured as of the time of the hazard event.
   *p is .05 or less.
  **p is .01 or less.
 ***p is .001 or less.

Household characteristics did not account for very much in affecting the probability of being contacted or receiving aid. Older households were less likely to receive aid, but the coefficient is so small, despite its significance, that a difference of 30 years between two households results in a corresponding difference of only .08 in the probability of receiving any help. More affluent households were also less likely to be contacted or to receive aid. In this case as well, the differences are not very large: A difference of $30,000 in annual household income resulted in an accompanying difference of .08 in the probability of receiving aid. The other coefficients are not significant, indicating that renters as compared with owners, whites as compared with blacks, and the highly educated compared with the less well educated, all had about the same probability of receiving aid.

The differences at the extremes, however, if we take into account hazard type and other characteristics, were quite large. For example, a household struck by a fire that caused $5,000 worth of damage, headed by a 25-year-old earning $15,000 a year, had a probability of .93 of receiving some aid or being contacted by an agency or receiving insurance payments. In contrast, a household that was headed by a 70-year-old who earned $40,000 a year and that received $200 damage in an earthquake had a probability of .07 of receiving aid.

The nonfindings shown in the regression analysis are at least as important as the statistically significant ones. For many years, there has been a concern expressed in the disaster relief community that existing relief mechanisms may be so sporadic or stochastic in their coverage that whole classes of the victimized population are simply lost. To prevent this problem, for example, the Red Cross frequently undertakes door-to-door canvassing, in the hope of finding individuals in need who would otherwise go unassisted. Many of the expressed concerns involve social inequities: It is sometimes maintained, for example, that only a relatively sophisticated individual can successfully navigate the "red tape" of receiving disaster relief assistance. This line of concern appears, on the basis of our data, to be completely unfounded.

Although it is true that some of our respondents who were victims of serious events (on the order of 15%) were never contacted by any help-giving agency, by far the largest bulk of them differed from those who were contacted mainly in the amount of damage incurred. Given the circumstances in which these agencies must operate (generalized chaos would not be an inappropriate description of the conditions obtaining in the immediate aftermath of a serious disaster), the coverage achieved was at worst commendable, and perhaps remarkable.

Hazard Aftermaths

No matter how slight the experience or how trivial the event, a hazard event is at least important enough to be remembered. Even the most trivial occurrence can have its effects for a short time as the household cleans up the debris of damage or waits for utilities to be restored. For more serious events, the aftermath can be more extended, requiring in some cases extensive repairs to property and persons. Where a household has had to borrow funds for repairs, the aftermath may be an increased debt burden or a prolonged discomfort.

Some of the aftermath effects of hazard experiences are shown in Table 6.17. As Section A indicates, one in four of the households experiencing serious events claimed to have suffered from an increased debt burden. The proportion claiming such increases varied from 45% of those involved in a serious flood event to none who were involved in minor earthquakes. Undoubtedly, the high damages inflicted by floods in conjunction with the low level of insurance coverage produced the experienced increase in debt burden for the flood victims.

A slightly higher proportion (29%) reported that they felt "depressed" after the event, as Section B indicates.[11] Again, serious

---

[11]Clearly, this is not a clinical diagnosis based on skillful observation; rather, it is the response to one item and, at best, a self-diagnosis. Nor were the intensity or duration of the "depressed" feelings indicated.

TABLE 6.17
Hazard-Event Aftermath-Effects by Hazard Type and Seriousness

Aftermath measure	Fire	Flood	Hurricane	Tornado	Earthquake	Combined hazards
A. Debt burden score[a]						
Serious events (percent)						
0	75	55	77	83	81	76
1–2	17	35	19	14	15	18
3+	8	10	4	3	4	6
Minor events (percent)						
0	100	93	100	99	100	99
1+	0	7	0	1	0	1
B. Felt depressed in aftermath[b]						
Serious events (percent)	39	45	22	22	20	29
Minor events (percent)	11	11	0	3	4	4
C. Time to complete repairs[c]						
Serious events						
Up to one day (percent)	20	26	40	40	67	35
Average number of days	40	46	28	19	10	31
Minor events						
Up to one day (percent)	92	96	95	94	99	96

	1	1	0	2	1	1
Average number of days						
D. Time to restoration of *Status quo*[d]						
Serious events (percent)						
Up to one day	18	7	23	36	36	26
1–7 days	15	22	19	23	14	20
8–28 days	19	27	24	18	20	21
More than 28 days	47	44	33	23	30	34
Minor events (percent)						
Up to one day	78	89	69	69	75	73
1–7 days	7	7	14	8	2	6
8–28 days	2	0	4	4	e	2
More than 28 days	13	4	13	19	23	19
Approximate N's						
Serious	(223)	(125)	(144)	(356)	(59)	(907)
Minor	(45)	(27)	(117)	(225)	(304)	(718)

[a]Based on a count of the number of positive ("yes") answers to the following set of questions: "As a result of the event, did any of the following happen to you or your family?
Going into debt to pay for medical bills
Going into debt to pay bills for repairs to property or for replacement of things destroyed
Being unemployed for more than a week because of damage to the place where you worked
Using up savings to pay for losses and expenses
Having to get an additional mortgage (or a bigger mortgage) to finance repairs to your house
Going into debt so deeply to pay for damages and/or injuries that you had to go without a lot of necessities to pay back your debts."
[b]Based on positive answers to the following question (in the same series as those in footnote a above): "Becoming depressed over the event."
[c]Based on how long it took family to repair damage to property.
[d]Based on answers to question "All told, how long did it take you and your family to settle back into your routine, after the event—how many days?"
[e]Less than 1%.

flood victims were more likely to claim this effect (45%), whereas at the other extreme few (1%) of the minor earthquake events were accompanied by feelings of being "depressed." Judged by the incidence of "depressed" feelings, the most serious hazard events were serious floods, followed by serious fires (39%), with the remaining hazards showing levels of "depression" around 20%. None of the minor events showed an incidence level higher than 11% and then only for fires and floods.

Displacement or lack of accommodations of one sort or another may be regarded as another aftermath problem. Damage to a home or an apartment may require going some time without the full set of the household amenities to which one has become accustomed. Indeed, repairs to housing as an aftermath of a serious hazard event quite often required a number of days to complete, the average for serious events being 31 days (or one month). Minor hazard events required only minimal amounts of time for the completion of repairs, 96% requiring less than a day for repairs.

Of course, making repairs is only part of the upset after a disaster. Employment may be interrupted, lost articles need to be replaced, and so on. We asked each of the respondents how long it took their household to return to its ordinary routine of living; the answers are shown in Section D. For one out of three households suffering a serious event, the restoration of the *status quo* took four weeks or more, varying with the type of event from almost half of the fire victims to less than one in four of the tornado victims. Most (almost three out of four) of the victims of minor events took less than a day to return to the routines of everyday life.

The regression equations in Table 6.18 explore the issue of what causes felt debt burdens and feelings of depression. The debt burden index and depressed feelings measures of Table 6.17 were used as dependent variables, with the independent variables being the hazard event and the household characteristics. Note that a positive coefficient means that the variable in question increased the sense of debt burden or of feelings of depression.

TABLE 6.18

Regressions of Hazard Aftermath Effects on Hazard and Household
Characteristics (N = 1,268)

Independent variables	Dependent variable			
	Debt burden index[a]		Depression[b]	
	b	SE	b	SE
Hazard type[c]				
Fire	−.0632	(.073)	.0160	(.035)
Flood	−.0023	(.081)	−.0064	(.034)
Hurricane	−.0946	(.065)	−.0850**	(.032)
Tornado	−.0671	(.055)	−.0329	(.027)
Hazard characteristics				
Damage to household[d]	.0771***	(.014)	.0350***	(.006)
Percentage reimbursed by insurance	−.0042***	(.001)	−.0013***	(.000)
Community seriousness[e]	−.0966***	(.023)	−.0219*	(.011)
Public service disruption[f]	.1186***	(.016)	.0132	(.008)
Repairs to home[g]	−.0110	(.051)	.0681**	(.025)
Restoration time[h]	.1342***	(.025)	.0876***	(.012)
Contacts with agencies[i]	.0749***	(.017)	.0322***	(.008)
Informal help[j]	.0554**	(.020)	.0267**	(.010)
Gifts/grants ($000)	.0085	(.017)	.0085	(.008)
Loans ($000)	.0077***	(.002)	−.0004	(.001)
Household characteristics				
Age of oldest person	−.0005	(.013)	−.0002	(.001)
Household income[k]	−.0074***	(.002)	−.0019*	(.001)
Renter	−.1502**	(.048)	.0264	(.024)
Number of persons	.0093	(.012)	.0008	(.006)
Education (years)	.0057	(.008)	.0001	(.004)
White	−.0045	(.051)	.0120	(.025)
Intercept	.1254	(.146)	.0531	(.071)
R^2 =	.35		.32	

[a]Index consisting of items on felt debt burden as aftermath of hazard event (see Table 6.17 for wording of questions).
[b]Answers to item "Becoming depressed over the event."
[c]Dummy variables: Omitted category is "earthquake."
[d]Coded in categories (see Table 6.2 for brackets used).
[e]Seriousness of event to community, consisting of amount of damage to other homes on block, in neighborhood, and in community.
[f]Number of interruptions to public services and utilities.
[g]Whether repair to home took up to one day to accomplish or greater.
[h]Length of time to restoration of "normal" activities of household.
[i]Number of agencies that contacted household.
[j]Number of informal sources providing help to household.
[k]Income measured as of year of the hazard event.
  *$p \leq .05$
 **$p \leq .01$
***$p \leq .001$

If we turn first to the debt burden equation, it is fairly obvious that the kind of hazard involved was not as important as the consequences of the hazards and the concomitant events. None of the coefficients for hazard types are significant, indicating that the hazards were not sufficiently different from each other in the net effects that they had on felt debt burden. However, the next set of variables did have important effects. First of all, the greater the dollar value of the damage inflicted, the greater the debt burden. Second, as expected, the larger the proportion of the damage reimbursed by insurance, the less the debt burden. Third, communitywide disasters led to less of a sense of debt burden. It may well be that when many face the same problems, one's own problems are reduced in magnitude. An alternative explanation is that in such widespread disasters, some of the burdens are assumed by others. In any event, it appears that the hazard event in which a household is one of a small number of victims leads to worse consequences than when there are many who share the same problems.

Fourth, it appears that the events involving the disruption of services and utilities led to greater debt burden. It is difficult to give a completely satisfactory explanation for this finding. Perhaps it means that when public services and utilities are disrupted, other economic side effects occur—including interruptions in employment[12] or reduced economic well-being for the community—that make it difficult for the household to sustain its debt payments.

Fifth, although whether repairs to the home took more than a minimal amount of time did not seem to matter to the feeling of debt burden, the length of time taken to restore the routines of the *status quo ante* did. The longer it took for a household to return to its regular ways of life, the greater the debt burden that was felt.

Sixth, contacts with relief agencies and receiving help from

---

[12]Note that one of the items that made up the debt burden index concerns whether the household had experienced unemployment of more than one week's duration.

informal sources both increased the sense of debt burden. It is also difficult to explain these findings. One might more easily assume the opposite: That the more help received and the more contacts with relief agencies, the more easily a household can carry the aftermath economic effects. However, the findings indicate that exact opposite. Of course, the formulation may misspecify the causal direction. Perhaps it was the debt burden (or its prospect) that led a family to seek information about aid and to seek help from friends, neighbors, and relatives. In any event, it is not possible[13] to unravel what is undoubtedly a very entangled web of cause and effect in the relationships between felt debt burden and these two variables.

Seventh, the larger the loans taken out by a household, the greater the debt burden felt—an obvious relationship. Note that gifts and grants did not have a discernible effect on debt burden.

Among the characteristics of households, only two turned out to be significant. The higher a household's income, the lower the felt debt burden—also a quite understandable finding. Renters also had less felt debt burden than owners.

The entire equation has a rather high R^2 (.35), indicating that more than a third of the variation in felt debt burden is explained by the variables included in the equation.

The pattern of coefficients for feelings of depression is some-what different. First, one of the hazard types was accompanied by a lowered level of depression: Hurricanes apparently significantly lowered the sense of depression (in comparison with earth-quakes), although the reasons for this effect are not apparent. It remains a mystery, especially when one keeps in mind that many things about the hazard experience are being held constant in the equation.

Second, as in the case of debt burden, the greater the damage

---

[13]Under some circumstances, it might have been possible to separate out the mutual effects of being in trouble and seeking aid, but this data set severely limited those possibilities. Several formulations of mutually interacting simultaneous equation models were tried, but the problems of endogeneity could not be overcome.

and the smaller the insurance reimbursement, the more likely were depressed feelings. Third, indicators of disruption also affected depressed feelings: Household repairs that took more than a minimal time, and the time it took to restore the *status quo ante*, were both related to depressed feelings.

Fourth, contacts with agencies and receiving help from informal sources increased the probability of claiming depressed feelings. Again, we are confronted with a finding that is difficult to interpret. Of course, as before, the causal direction may be mistaken, with depressed persons seeking out agencies and aid from friends and neighbors.

Among the characteristics of households, only income seems to have affected feelings of being depressed. The greater the income at the time of the event, the less likely was a household to claim having been depressed by the event.

All told, a little less than a third of the variation in depressed feelings is explained by the equation ($R^2 = .32$). From the patterning of the coefficients, it is obvious that the characteristics of the disaster event were the main determinants of depression. When the event was traumatic and had serious effects on the household, it admitted to being depressed by the event.

SUMMARY

The large average losses sustained in damaging hazard events, as discussed in the previous chapter, are clearly offset to an important extent by patterns of aid and financial relief. For hazards other than flood and earthquake, private insurance is, assuredly, the first line of defense. In the case of floods and earthquakes (and in the other hazard types to a lesser extent), various federal and private relief agencies are an important secondary presence, and many state and local groups and agencies are also involved. Finally, when all else fails, most victims can rely on family and friends for needed moral and financial support.

Although no single agency or group makes contact with a

large share of the total victim population, the aggregate contact for all groups considered together is indeed quite large. Most victims of serious hazard events are contacted by at least one help-giving agency; and most of the victims contacted reported a high degree of satisfaction with the services received. The various sources of aid available appear to play quite complementary roles: Households whose losses are not covered by insurance, for example, usually find other sources of assistance to which they can turn. In most cases, the amount of help received is correlated with the amount of loss incurred, and with little else. There is no evidence anywhere in the chapter to suggest gross inequities in the distribution of hazard-relief services.

Beyond the immediate losses, hazard events have various other consequences, none of which have been examined here. A fairly substantial fraction of our victims of serious events claimed an increased debt burden as a result, and many (about one-third) also reported being depressed. On the average, home repairs following serious events took about a month to complete. These *sequelae* notwithstanding, most households, even those victimized by serious events, claimed to have returned to their normal routines in a matter of a few weeks. The relatively short "recovery time" reported by our respondents may have been a direct consequence of the coverage achieved by the various help-giving groups and agencies, but it was assuredly a testament to the resiliency of the American population.

References

American National Red Cross. *Annual Summaries of Disaster Services Activities*, ANRC National Office, mimeographed. 1959–1977.

Brinkman, Waltraud A. R. *Severe Local Storm Hazard in the United States: A Research Assessment*. Boulder, Colo.: Institute of Behavioral Science Monograph, #NSF-RA-E-75-11. 1975.

Cochrane, Harold L. *Natural Hazards and Their Distributive Effects*. Boulder, Colo.: Institute of Behavioral Sciences Monograph, #NSF-RA-E-75-003. 1975.

Comptroller General of the United States. *California Drought of 1976 and 1977—Extent, Damage, and Governmental Response*. Washington, D.C.: General Accounting Office, 1977.

Dacy, D. C. and Kunreuther, H. *The Economics of Natural Disasters: Implications for Federal Policy*. New York: Free Press, 1969.

Dillman, D. A. *Mail and Telephone Surveys*. New York: Wiley, 1978.

Federal Emergency Management Administration, *Special Statistical Summary*, Washington, D.C.: Federal Emergency Management Administration, 1982.

Groves, R. M., and Kahn, R. L. *Surveys by Telephone: A National Comparison with Personal Interviews*. New York: Academic Press, 1978.

Herbert, P. J., and Taylor, G. *Hurricane Experience Levels of Coastal County Populations—Texas to Maine*. U.S. Department of Commerce, National Oceanic and Atmospheric Administration, 1975.

Kunreuther, H., et al. *Limited Knowledge and Insurance Protection: Implications for Natural Hazard Policy*. Philadelphia: Wharton School, University of Pennsylvania. Draft report (mimeographed). 1977.

National Fire Prevention and Control Agency, *The National Household Fire Survey*, Washington, D.C.: Federal Emergency Management Administration, 1977.

National Oceanic and Atmospheric Administration. *Johnstown, Pennsyl-*

vania Flash Flood of July 19–20, 1977: A Report to the Administrator. Washington, D.C.: U.S. Government Printing Office, 1977.

Office of Management and Budget. *The United States Budget in Brief: FY 1978.* Washington, D.C.: U.S. Government Printing Office, 1978.

Rossi, P. H., Wright, J. D., et al. *Natural Hazards and Public Choice: The State and Local Politics of Hazard Mitigation.* New York: Academic Press, 1982.

U.S. Department of Commerce. *Statistical Abstract of the United States.* Washington, D.C.: U.S. Government Printing Office, 1973.

Warrick, R. A. *Drought Hazard in the United States: A Research Assessment.* Boulder, Colo.: Institute of Behavioral Science Monograph, #NSF-RA-E-75-004. 1975.

White, G. F., and Haas, E. J. *Assessment of Research on Natural Hazards.* Cambridge, Mass.: M.I.T. Press, 1975.

Wright, J. D., Rossi, P. H., et al. *The Apathetic Politics of Natural Disasters.* Amherst, Mass.: Social and Demographic Research Institute (mimeographed). 1979a.

Wright, J. D., Rossi, P. H., Wright, S. R., and Weber-Burdin, E. *After the Clean-Up: Long Range Effects of Natural Disasters.* Beverly Hills, Calif.: Sage, 1979b.

Wright, H. D., and Rossi, P. H. (Eds.), *Social Science and Natural Hazards,* Cambridge, Mass.: Abt Books, 1982.

Estimates of Victimization and Losses Based on Pre-1980 Data

In order to properly design the national survey described in this volume, it was necessary to develop the best possible estimates of the proportions of households experiencing each of the hazards studied and of the accompanying damages. The estimates were to be used in calculating the necessary sample size for the contemplated telephone survey. Constructing the estimates was a laborious task that had the surprising (at least to the investigators) outcome of converging on a relatively firm set of numbers. Although we did not have any *a priori* expectation that these estimates would be close to those arising from the survey later conducted, the convergence was close enough to raise the level of confidence in both sets of estimates.

We reproduce the design estimates in this appendix because we believe that readers may want to verify for themselves that the survey estimates are not far afield from what other data lead one to expect. It should be noted that these estimates were computed in 1979 and based in some cases on data that were collected in earlier years. Hence, the monetary estimates are in deflated dollars and would need to be corrected to some constant dollar base to be comparable with our own survey findings. However, dollar estimates were not as important for our survey design purposes as incidence estimates: Hence, the numbers given below are in uninflated dollars.

HAZARD VICTIMIZATION BY AGENT: EXISTING ESTIMATES (AS OF 1979)

In order to design and budget the victimization survey, it was essential to know, as precisely as possible, how many screening interviews would be required to produce "enough" victims of the various hazards to sustain a meaningful analysis. With the loose criterion of "nontrivial" losses and a time frame of 10 years, what did the existing information base (as of 1979) suggest about victimization rates?

FIRE

So far as we could determine, there were three existing estimates of the rate of victimization by fire. The first was contained in survey data generated by the Social and Demographic Research Institute in California in the summer of 1977 (we will call this the *California survey*; see Rossi et al., 1982: Ch. 5, for results from the survey); the second was contained in the American National Red Cross *Annual Summaries of Disaster Services Activities* for the years 1970 through 1977; the third was the National Household Fire Survey conducted for the National Fire Prevention and Control Administration.

The California survey asked respondents, "Have you ever personally experienced a serious forest or brush fire, either in your present community or elsewhere?" In all, 18.2% of the respondents answered "yes." As an estimate of the national rate of victimization from fires, this number was judged as probably too high for at least four reasons:

1. The question asked whether the respondent had *ever* experienced a fire and thus posed no specific time frame for the response. As *ever* presumably means "in your lifetime," and as the average age of the respondents in this survey was about 40 years, the 18.2% figure should therefore be divided by about 4 to yield an estimate of fire victimization *in any 10-year period*. With this correction, a more reasonable incidence figure of about 4.5% resulted.
2. Further, the question asked whether the respondents had ever *experienced* a fire, not whether they had actually suffered loss. The proportion who had suffered a loss presumably would have been smaller than the proportion ever experiencing a fire.
3. The survey in question was conducted in California, where forest and brush fires are more common than in the nation at large.

4. And finally, the survey was conducted in the summer of 1977, when much of California was ablaze.

On the other hand, the estimate from the California survey was probably too low for at least one reason: It asked only about forest and brush fires, not about other kinds of fires (home fires, arson, electrical fires, etc.). Assuming that underestimation due to this last point would have approximately offset the overestimation due to Points 2 through 4, we arrived at an estimated fire victimization rate for the nation at large during a 10-year period of roughly 5%.

Data from the National Household Fire Survey suggested a very similar victimization rate. The survey was based on a very large sample of about 33,000 households, among which a total of 2,463 "fire incidents" were reported. Assuming one fire incident per household (a liberal assumption, obviously), this total translated into an estimated victimization rate of 7.5% (2,463/33,000 = .075). However, only 1,070 of the reported incidents actually resulted in material losses to the victims, a nontrivial victimization rate on the order of 3.2%, which was respectably close to the estimate generated from the California survey data. Unfortunately, we were not able to determine the time frame of the incident question used in the National Household Fire Survey: Hence, the comparison of results with other sources was very loose, at best.

The ANRC (American National Red Cross) annual summary data were more cumbersome to work with. The summaries provide disaster-specific detail (essential for our purposes) only for those disasters affecting five or more families, a relatively small subset of the disasters to which the Red Cross responds. For example, in fiscal year (FY) 1972–1973, the ANRC responded to a total of 25,273 disasters, of which 24,647 (97.5%) each involved fewer than five families. Thus, we had to make inferences about the characteristics of the vast majority of ANRC responses on the basis of the relatively small number of them for which detailed disaster-specific data are available.

Defining the ANRC disasters involving more than five families as "big hits," we found that for the years 1970–1977, the average annual number of big hits was 841, of which 645 were fire disasters. Thus, roughly three-quarters of all big hits represented fire disasters (the average proportion over the seven-year period was actually 76.03%). During the same period, the average annual number of "little hits" was 28,597. Assuming that similar proportions held for both big and little hits, the resulting estimate was that in the average years, 21,742 of the ANRC's little hits involved fire disasters (28,597 × .7603 = 21,742). Note that, if anything, this estimate is very likely low, because it can be assumed that most fire disasters are likely to be little hits (i.e., that the proportion of fire disasters among the little hits may be higher than 76%).

How many fire victims were represented in each of the big and little hits? For the big hits, an estimate could be extracted directly from the *Annual Summaries* data, which contained, among other pieces of information, an estimate (or more accurately, a "ballpark guess") of the "total number of families suffering loss" from the event in question. For the years 1970–1977, the annual average number of families suffering loss from fire in big hits was, according to the ANRC, 8,884 families (see Table A.1). To this figure must be added the number of families suffering loss in the little hits. A *little hit* was defined as involving five or fewer families: We assumed that the average little hit involves two families. The average annual number of families suffering fire losses in ANRC little hits could therefore be estimated at 2 × 21,742, or 43,484 families. The total number of families suffering loss in an average year from big and little hits combined was thus estimated to be 43,484 + 8,884, or 52,368 families. Because this estimate was an average for a *year*, it could be multiplied by 10 to produce an estimate for the average decade; our best estimate from the ANRC data was thus that roughly 523,700 families were victimized by fire in the average decade.

TABLE A.1

Victimization by Fire Hazard as Estimated from ANRC Annual Summaries of Disaster Services Activities, 1970–1977

Year	N of "big hits"	N of "big" fire hits	Percentage	N of "little hits"	N of "big hit" family victims
1976–1977	963	800	83.1	35,971	12,075
1975–1976	1,005	774	77.0	31,017	10,933
1974–1975	1,023	801	78.3	30,968	9,740
1973–1974	963	743	77.2	28,890	8,344
1972–1973	626	450	71.9	24,647	6,059
1971–1972	633	436	68.9	24,294	5,922
1970–1971	675	512	75.8	24,395	9,118
Mean	841	645	76.0	28,597	8,884

Calculation of final estimate
1. Average number of families victimized by "big hit" fires in any year   8,884
2. Average number of "little hit" fires in any year = .76 × 28,597 = 21,742
3. Average number of families affected by each "little hit" = 2 (by assumption)
4. Average number of families victimized by "little hit" fires in any year (2) × (3)   43,484
5. Total number of families victimized by fire in any given year (1) + (4)   52,368
6. Total number of families victimized by fire in any given decade (5) × 10 523,680

This figure could be expected to be too low for at least one reason: it represented families affected by fires *responded to by the ANRC*, which must have been somewhat less than the total number of fires that occurred. How much less, of course, could not be precisely determined.

There were approximately 251,000 residential fires in the United States according to the *Statistical Abstract of the United States* (U.S. Department of Commerce, 1973:467), or about five times more residential fires than the estimated number of families affected as determined from the ANRC data (251,000/52,368 = 4.79). Thus, perhaps no more than one in every five fire victims appears in the ANRC report data.

Ignoring for the moment the preceding point, recall that the ANRC data suggest about 523,700 family fire victims in an average decade. To transform this figure into a percentage, we divided by the number of households in the country, approximately 54,070,000 families during the period represented by the ANRC data. The resulting estimated victimization *rate* was therefore 523,700/54,070,000 = 0.97%, or 1% for all practical purposes. As the data from the preceding paragraph suggest, the ANRC data underestimated the true number of victims by a factor of as much as 5, and as the estimated rates from available survey data were in the range of 3%–5%, we felt reasonably confident in concluding that the "true" rate of victimization by fire hazard was on the order of 3%–5% for any given 10-year period. We chose 4% as the design estimate (i.e., the estimate on which to base our survey sample design).

FLOOD

Victimization rates for floods can be calculated from four sources: from the Social and Demographic Research Institute (SADRI) California survey, from the ANRC *Annual Summaries* data, from national survey data generated by the authors in the summer of 1977 (Wright et al., 1979a), and from the ANRC chapter report data for 1960–1970 as discussed in Wright et al. (1979b).

The California survey asked, "Have you ever personally experienced a serious flood, either in your present community or elsewhere?" The proportion responding "yes" was 25.0%. Correction for average age produced an estimate of about 6.25% per decade (25%/4 = 6.25%). As above, this estimate can be assumed to be too high (relative to the true national flood victimization rate) for three reasons: (1) As in the case of fires, "experienced" is not the same as "victimized"; (2) flood risk is higher in California than in the nation as a whole; and (3) the nine communities sampled in the California survey were sampled with probabilities proportionate to the total population at risk (PPPR) from floods, hurricanes, tornadoes, and earthquakes (see Rossi et al., 1982, for a discussion of the sampling rationale); as a result, the resulting flood (and earthquake) victimization estimates were somewhat high relative to the true victimization rate even in California, let alone in the nation at large. Of these reasons (1) is probably the most serious; on its account alone, we can reduce the net estimate to perhaps 4%.

The national "key persons" survey (KPS) (Rossi et al., 1982) asked, "Have you ever personally experienced a flood, either here or elsewhere?" The proportion responding "yes" to this question was 56.4%. The mean age of respondents in the KPS survey was 48.2 years; the ensuing correction thus produced a figure of 12.2% victimized by flood in any given decade (56.4%/4.82 = 12.2%).

For those reporting a flood experience, a KPS follow-up question asked, "During what year did you experience that flood?" With this question, it was possible to generate decade-by-decade experience rates. In all, 12.2% of the sample reported a flood experience during the 1950s, 12.8% during the 1960s, and 16.8% during the 1970s. (Reported experiences for decades prior to the 1950s were substantially lower.) The average of these three figures is 13.9%, very close to the 12.2% figure produced by the age correction in the previous paragraph. The close agreement between estimates therefore increased confidence in the meaningfulness of the age corrections required in the California survey.

As in the California survey, the KPS question asked about "experience," not directly about victimization. However, for respondents reporting a flood experience, a second follow-up question asked, "Did you or your family suffer any property losses or personal injuries as a result of the flood?" In all, 27.8% of those reporting a flood experience answered "yes" to the follow-up question. Our best estimate of the proportion truly victimized by flood was therefore 13.9% (the mean percentage experiencing a flood in any decade) times .278 (the proportion of those experiencing a flood who actually suffered loss), or 3.86%. For convenience, we rounded off to a simple 4% flood victimization rate, or about the same rate suggested in the California data.

As an estimate of the national flood victimization rate, the KPS estimate of 4% per decade could be assumed to be too high for at least two reasons. First, the states and local communities surveyed in the KPS were again sampled PPPR; the flood victimization among respondents from these states and communities was therefore probably higher than would be observed in a simple probability sample of the nation. And second, the persons interviewed in the KPS were drawn disproportionately from positions having direct hazard-related interests or responsibilities, which might suggest that they were also more likely to have had disaster experiences.

As for the second of these problems, little or nothing could be done; as for the first, however, it was possible to weight the KPS sample by the inverse of the sampling fraction for each state and to reconstruct the victimization estimates. The resulting *weighted* KPS data yielded results very similar to those from the unweighted data reported above. Specifically, the gross "experience" rate for the total weighted sample was 54.0% (vs. 56.4%); the average rate of flood experience by decade was 13.0% (vs. 13.9%); the proportion of those experiencing a flood who suffered loss was 28.2% (vs. 27.8%); and the resulting "best guess" estimate of true flood victimization in any decade was 3.67% (vs. 3.86% for the unweighted data). Both weighted and unweighted data thus suggest about 4% as the correct flood-victimization rate.

Following the procedures discussed earlier regarding fires, we found that the ANRC *Annual Summaries* data also produced estimates of flood victimization. The data and arithmetic are shown in Table A.2. Our best estimate from these data was that 655,750 families were victimized by flood in the average decade; division by 54,070,000, the total number of

TABLE A.2
Victimization by Flood as Estimated from ANRC Annual Summaries of Disaster Services Activities, 1970–1977

Year	N of "big hits"	N of "big" fire hits	Percentage	N of "little hits"	N of "big hit" family victims
1976–1977	963	58	6.0	35,971	45,690
1975–1976	1,005	70	7.0	31,017	34,968
1974–1975	1,023	90	8.8	30,968	26,700
1973–1974	963	83	8.6	28,890	35,189
1972–1973	626	78	12.5	24,647	99,245
1971–1972	633	77	12.2	24,294	156,541
1970–1971	675	49	7.3	24,395	25,018
Mean	841	72	8.9	28,597	60,479

Calculation of final estimate
1. Average number of families victimized by "big hit" floods in any year........ 60,479
2. Average number of "little hit" floods in any year = .0891 × 28,597 = 2,548
3. Average number of families affected by each "little hit" = 2 (by assumption)
4. Average number of families victimized by "little hit" floods in any year (2) × (3).. 5,096
5. Total number of families victimized by flood in any given year (1) + (4) 65,575
6. Total number of families victimized by flood in any given decade (5) × 10.... 655,750

families, produced an estimated victimization rate of 1.21%. As above, this number was probably too low for at least two reasons. First, it reflected only the floods to which the ANRC responded, which must be a subset of all floods; and second, the victimization count was based only on the victims known to the ANRC, which in turn must be a subset of all victims.

A final estimate, also based on Red Cross data, was derived from data reported in Wright et al. (1979b). These data consist of machine-readable information coded from ANRC chapter reports for the years 1960 through 1970. Rather than the cumbersome estimations required for the *Annual Summaries* data, these data can be manipulated more directly; that is, one simply sums the total number of families affected by floods across all reports for all 10 years, then divides by the total number of families in the country. When we used the 1960 value for the total number of families, the resulting victimization estimate was 1.12%; when we used the 1970 value, the estimate was 1.08%. Note that both values are very close to the *Annual Summaries* estimate of 1.21%.

Thus, the ANRC data converged on an estimated flood victimization rate per decade of about 1%, and the survey data converged on an estimate of about 4%. We gave more weight to the survey data for two reasons: first, like all agency data, the ANRC data were known to be incomplete; and second, the "victimization" questions from the two surveys were prototypes of questions to be asked in the proposed research. Still, as an estimate of the national flood rate, the 4% figure was probably somewhat high; we thus chose 3% as the design estimate.

HURRICANES

Three sources of data were available for estimates of victimization by hurricane: the KPS national survey data, the 1960–1970 ANRC Chapter Report data, and some inferential estimates supplied by Hebert and Taylor (1975:4). The California survey did not include a question on hurricanes; likewise, the ANRC *Annual Summaries* data could not be used because in some years there was no separate tally of hurricane data.

The KPS survey asked, "Have you ever personally experienced a hurricane, either here or elsewhere?" The proportion responding "yes" was 60.0% for the unweighted data and 57.7% for the weighted data. Correction of both these estimates for the average age of the sample gave values of 12.4% and 12.0%, respectively. For the past three decades, the average percentage experiencing a hurricane per decade was 13.9% and

13.5%, respectively, for unweighted and weighted data. Thus, all KPS estimates of the rate of hurricane experience converged on values in the range of 12%–14%.

The percentage of those experiencing a hurricane who actually suffered losses was 37.8% for the unweighted data and 39.1% for the weighted data. Our best unweighted estimate of the rate of hurricane victimization was therefore 13.9% × .378, or 5.25%. The corresponding value for weighted data was 5.27%. Rounding down, we arrived at a value of about 5% of the nation suffering loss from hurricane in any given decade.

The 1960–1970 ANRC Chapter Report data, as always, produced lower estimates than those produced by the KPS. When we used the 1960 value for the total number of families in the denominator, the ANRC estimate of hurricane victimization was 1.52% per decade; when we used the 1970 value, the estimate was 1.36%. For all the usual reasons, it could be assumed that these figures were somewhat lower than the true hurricane victimization rate.

Because not all parts of the nation are equally susceptible to hurricane hazard, a revised set of estimates can be made on the basis of data just for the coastal states (Texas to Maine). Because 13 of the 20 states sampled in KPS were coastal states, the resulting victimization estimate was reasonably close to that shown in the total. Just in the coastal states, 74.4% of the respondents said that they had experienced a hurricane sometime during their lives (unweighted data), which corrects to 15.44% in any decade. The average "percentage experiencing a hurricane" by decade, likewise, was 18.3%, 40% of whom report having suffered at least some loss because of the hurricane. Among the coastal states, then, the resulting "best guess" estimate for hurricane victimization in any decade was 7.32% (18.3% × .400 = 7.32%), or roughly 7%, for convenience.

The ANRC Chapter Report data can also be broken down by state; when we used the 1970 estimate of total number of families in the coastal states, the resulting hurricane victimization estimate for families in the coastal states was 4.22% per decade.

Hebert and Taylor, via indirect and inferential methods, calculated that 77.5% of the population who were currently residents in the coastal states had never experienced a direct hurricane hit. Thus, 22.5% of the population presumably had. If we assume that the average age of the adult population of the coastal states was about 45 years, the estimated per decade victimization by hurricane based on the Hebert–Taylor figure was therefore 5.0% (22.5%/4.5 = 5.0%).

Overall, then, the high estimate for hurricane victimization per decade in the nation at large was about 5% (KPS), and the low estimate was about 1.5% (ANRC). Thus, our "best guess" estimate of the true national hurricane victimization rate was on on the order of 3%. Just for the coastal states, we had estimates of about 4% (ANRC), about 5% (Hebert and Taylor), and about 7% (KPS); a reasonable guess is thus that the true value for the coastal states was about 5%.

TORNADOES

There were three sources of data that could be used in estimating the rate of victimization by tornado: the KPS survey, the ANRC *Annual Summaries*, and the ANRC Chapter Report data.

The KPS survey asked, "Have you ever personally experienced a tornado, either here or elsewhere?" The proportion responding "yes" was 35.6%, or roughly 7% for any given decade. (The weighted data give virtually identical results.) For the past three decades, the average percentage of the sample experiencing a tornado was 9.0%. Of those who had experienced a tornado, the proportion reporting that they had suffered some loss was 26.3%. Our best estimate of the true victimization rate for tornadoes is thus 9.0% × .263, or 2.36% overall.

Using the 1960 value for the total number of families in the country, the ANRC Chapter Report data showed an overall tornado victimization rate of 0.34%. When the 1970 value was substituted, the rate was 0.33%. Data for 1970–1977, taken from the *Annual Summaries* and manipulated as indicated in previous sections, produced a final estimate of victimization by tornado of 0.29%. Thus, all ANRC data converged on a rate of about 0.3% as the true rate of victimization by tornado per decade.

For all the usual reasons, the KPS estimate was probably somewhat high and the ANRC-based estimates were probably somewhat low. We chose 1% as the design estimate.

EARTHQUAKE

Because earthquakes, unlike the other disaster agents so far discussed, are not regular occurrences, and because earthquake risk is not proportionately distributed throughout the United States, it is very difficult to provide a meaningful estimate of the rate of victimization by earthquakes for the nation as a whole. The best data exist for the state of California, and it may well be that the rate of earthquake victimization can be calculated only for that state (as no other state has produced enough victims in any typical time-span to allow for the calculation of a rate).

The California survey asked, "Have you ever personally experienced a serious earthquake either in your present community or elsewhere?" The proportion responding "yes" to this question was 39.2%, or roughly 10% per decade. The proportion actually victimized by earthquake would, of course, be less.

The KPS survey asked all respondents, "Have you ever personally experienced an earthquake, either here or elsewhere?" In the total sample, 29.3% responded "yes," and among California respondents, the proportion was 87.9%. The average percentage experiencing an earthquake in any decade (computed during the past three decades) was 7.33% for the total sample and 23.0% for the California respondents. The follow-up question revealed that about 9.0% of those experiencing an earthquake were actually victimized by one (total sample); in California, the corresponding percentage was 14.8%. Thus, the best estimate for earthquake victimization in the nation at large is 7.33% $\times$ .090, or 0.6% overall.

OTHER HAZARD AGENTS

Data on victimization by hazard agents other than the five so far discussed are so sparse and imprecise as to preclude any firm estimates of victimization rates; thus, the numbers discussed in the next several paragraphs were regarded with considerable suspicion.

Four of the remaining hazard agents—hail, lightning, drought, and frost—are primarily, although not exclusively, problems in the agricultural sector. For convenience (and as a conservative assumption), then, we may simply assume that victimization by these four agents is restricted to the nation's farm population, which, in turn, represents about 4% of the total labor force of the country.

Hail. It has been estimated that approximately 2% of the annual crop production of the United States is destroyed by hail every year; the total dollar losses from hail (all sources combined) average about $700 million annually (Brinkman, 1975:69–75). Remote inferences from other data presented by Brinkman, 1975:72) further suggested that losses to the typical hail-victimized farmer amount to about 10% of that farmer's total crops. If so, then the implication is that about 20% of the American farm population is victimized by hail in any given year (20% each losing about 10% adds up to total losses of about 2% of total production). Taken to their extremes, these numbers also suggest that roughly 200% of the farm population is victimized by hail in any 10-year period (i.e., that the typical farmer is stricken twice by hail every 10 years). On the surface, this figure seemed implausibly high; let us therefore further assume that the "20% victimized" figure represents the *total* victimization for any typical decade. If 20% of the nation's farmers were in fact victimized by hail in any typical decade, and if farmers represented roughly 4% of the total population, then the resulting "best guess" estimate for hail victimization in the nation at large would be 4% × .20 = 0.8%. We chose 0.5% as the "best guess" design estimate.

Drought.   Warrick (1975:xiv) suggested that $700 million annually "can be considered reasonable" as the average crop losses due to drought in any "typical" year. This is the same average-loss figure that Brinkmann suggested for hail (see previous paragraph). If we assume that the victimization from each hazard is proportional to the loss, we can draw the inference that victimization by drought is roughly equal to victimization by hail; we therefore took the 0.5% figure as a reasonable overall estimate of the rate of drought victimization. Note that because of the Great Western Drought of 1976–1977, this figure is likely to have been somewhat low.[1]

Annual crop losses from *frost and freezing* were estimated at about $1.1 billion (White and Haas, 1975:305). Because this was about the same figure as shown above for hail and drought, we assumed that victimization was proportional to loss and produced an estimate of the rate of victimization by frost and freezing of roughly 0.5%.

Lightning.   Brinkman (1975:106) reported that "two out of every 100 farms are struck by lightning or have a fire (which may be lightning-caused) each year." The implication is that 20 farms in every 100 are victimized by lightning in any decade; thus, a reasonable guess about overall lightning victimization was 20% × 4% (the proportion of farmers), or 0.8%. Here too, then, we may assume that the true rate of lightning victimization is on the order of 0.5% of the nation's families in any typical decade.

Taking these four hazard agents combined, then, we arrive at an overall victimization rate of about 2%. This figure suggests that approximately one-half the nation's farms suffer some nontrivial loss from hail,

[1]The KPS survey asked respondents whether "within the last ten years" drought had been a problem in their respective states or local communities. Overall, 54.4% responded "yes" to this question. This response suggests at least the possibility that the drought victimization estimate provided in this paragraph is *much* too low. The same question sequence was also asked about "hailstorms"; the proportion saying these had been a problem in their states or communities in the last 10 years was 22.5%. If we assume constant proportionalities, the drought estimate suggests that drought victimization may average twice that of victimization by hail; that is, the correct figure for drought may be closer to 1.0% than to 0.5%.

drought, frost, or lightning in the average decade, and this did not seem to be an unreasonably high estimate. Further, our estimate for at least one hazard, drought, could have been substantially too low; and also, it was clearly *not* the case that victimization from these four hazards was exclusively restricted to the agricultural sector. Thus, an overall rate of about 2% per decade for these four agents combined seems at least plausible.

The remaining hazard agents that we considered are coastal erosion, severe windstorm (other than tornado or hurricane), landslide, and blizzard. The available numerical data on these four agents consisted primarily of order-of-magnitude estimates of the total annual dollar losses. In the cases of hail, drought, and frost, we have assumed (implicitly) that annual losses of about $1 billion translate into a victimization rate over a decade of about 0.5%. We took the simple assumption that this ratio also held for the remaining four agents. White and Haas (1975:361) estimated that losses from coastal erosion average about $300 million per year, yielding an estimated victimization rate of 0.15%. Losses from severe windstorms (other than tornadoes and hurricanes) were estimated at between $30 million and $300 million annually (White and Haas, 1975:299); the midpoint of this interval is $165 million, which translated into a victimization rate of roughly 0.08%. The annual loss from landslides was estimated at "hundreds of millions of dollars annually" (White and Haas, 1975:339). The assumption that loss from landslides did not exceed loss from erosion and windstorm combined (i.e., that the loss was on the order of $500 million annually) in turn suggested a victimization rate of roughly 0.25%.

As for "urban snow," no cost figures are provided. The combined victimization from erosion, severe windstorm, and landslide was now estimated at 0.15% + 0.08% + 0.25%, or 0.48% overall; simply asserting (on the basis of no evidence whatsoever) that victimization by urban blizzard runs to about 0.5% has the convenient effect of producing an overall estimate of about 1% as the proportion of the nation's families victimized by erosion, landslide, severe windstorm, or blizzard in any typical decade.[2]

---

[2]The KPS survey included "snowfall" in the question sequence discussed in the previous footnote. In all, 31.4% of the respondents said that this had been a problem, a slightly higher proportion than responded "yes" to the question on hail. If we assume constant proportions once again, and if we assume further that our guess on hail victimization is not totally unreasonable, the true rate of victimization by blizzard may be as high as 1.0%. The very severe blizzards of the winters of 1976–1977 and 1977–1978 may mean that the actual rate over the previous decade was substantially higher than even this 1% figure.

At the point of drawing up the actual design of the telephone survey, we reviewed these estimates and came to the conclusion that those pertaining to coastal erosion, windstorms, landslides, and blizzards were simply too conjectural to use. In addition, even the highest estimates yielded proportions that indicated that finding sufficient numbers of households that had been victimized to the point of suffering nontrivial losses was going to be extremely expensive. As a consequence, we dropped these hazard events from our study and concentrated mainly on household fires, floods, hurricanes, tornadoes, and earthquakes, being fully confident only that we could obtain sufficient numbers of victims from the first four to sustain the kinds of analyses we contemplated. We included earthquakes (broadening the definition to include tremors) without much confidence that we would be able to carry through a meaningful analysis. As the reader of the preceding chapters may have noted, the analysis of earthquake victims often rests on precariously small case bases, as we had feared.

SUMMARY

Table A.3 summarizes the victimization estimates generated in the previous pages. Our design estimate for the overall rate of individual or

TABLE A.3
Summary of Disaster Victimization Estimates for Total U.S. Population

Disaster agent	High estimate (%)	Low estimate (%)	Design estimate (%)
Fire	5	1.0	4
Flood	4	1.1	3
Hurricane	5	1.5	3
Tornado	2	0.3	1
Earthquake	0.7	—	0.5
Hail			
Drought			
Frost	—	—	2
Lightning			
Blizzard			
Severe windstorm	—	—	1
Landslide			
Erosion			
Total = 14.5			

family victimization from all agents combined for the typical decade was 14.5%, or roughly 15% for convenience. As Chapter 4 indicates, the design estimates were quite close to the actual yields of victims in the national telephone survey, the differences being mainly generated by slightly changed definitions of the hazards involved. For example, we included windstorms with tornadoes, tremors with earthquakes, and severe tropical storms with hurricanes, all threshold changes that tended to yield more instances in our victimization survey than were predicted in the design estimates.

APPENDIX B

Questionnaires Used in the National Telephone Survey and the Mailed Survey of Hazard Victims

Respondent's Name _____

Address _____
          (Street)   (City)   (State)   (Zip)

Telephone (_____) _____
         Area Code

AUDITS & SURVEYS, INC.   PROJECT No. 4278
One Park Avenue   November 1980
New York, N.Y. 10016

NATURAL HAZARDS STUDY

SCREENER

Interviewer's Name (Print) _____

Time of Call _____   Date _____

INTRODUCTION

Hello, I'm _____ of Audits & Surveys, a national market research firm located in New York City. May I speak to the male or female head of household?

If head of household is unavailable, make appointment for callback on call record form.

If head of household is then put on the phone, repeat:

Hello, I'm _____ of Audits & Surveys, a national market research firm located in New York City.

Continued Introduction to Head of Household

At the request of the University of Massachusetts, we are conducting a survey to obtain information on damages to individuals and families from events such as fires, floods, and other natural disasters. We would like to ask you a few questions regarding your family's experiences with such events during the past ten years, since 1970.

1. Since 1970, has your family or household   **Yes ( )   Ask Q. 2**
    experienced a fire in a house or apartment   **No ( )   Skip to Q. 7**
    in which you were living as a group?

If "Yes" in Q. 1, Ask:

2. In which year or years did the fire or fires occur? *Check all years that apply in column under Q. 2 below.*

    For Each Year Checked in Q. 2, Ask:

    3. Now, thinking about (*insert first year mentioned in Q. 2*) how many fires did your family or household experience during that year? *Enter number of fires in column under Q. 3 below.*

    4. Was anyone in your family or household killed as a result of injuries due to fire? *Enter "Yes" or "No" in column under Q. 4 below.*

    5. Was anyone (else) in your family or household injured seri-

ously enough to be treated medically? *Enter "Yes" or "No" in column under Q. 5 below.*

6. Please estimate the total dollar amount of fire damage. *Enter dollar damage in column under Q. 6 below.*

Repeat Q. 3, 4, 5, and 6 for all other years in which fires occurred.

Q. 2 Year	Q. 3 No. Fires	Q. 4 Killed		Q. 5 Injured		Q. 6 $ Damage
		Yes	No	Yes	No	
1970( )	_____	( )	( )	( )	( )	_____
1971( )	_____	( )	( )	( )	( )	_____
1972( )	_____	( )	( )	( )	( )	_____
1973( )	_____	( )	( )	( )	( )	_____
1974( )	_____	( )	( )	( )	( )	_____
1975( )	_____	( )	( )	( )	( )	_____
1976( )	_____	( )	( )	( )	( )	_____
1977( )	_____	( )	( )	( )	( )	_____
1978( )	_____	( )	( )	( )	( )	_____
1979( )	_____	( )	( )	( )	( )	_____
1980( )	_____	( )	( )	( )	( )	_____

7. Since 1970, has your family or household experienced a flood caused by the overflowing of a river or stream in a house or apartment in which you were living as a group?

Yes ( )   Ask Q. 8
No ( )   Skip to Q. 13

If "Yes" in Q. 7, Ask:

8. In which year or years did the flood or floods occur? *Check all years that apply in column under Q. 8 below.*

For Each Year Checked in Q. 8, Ask:

9. Now, thinking about (*insert first year mentioned in Q. 8*) how many floods did your family or household experience during that year? *Enter number of floods in column under Q. 9 below.*

10. Was anyone in your family or household killed as a result of injuries due to flood? *Enter "Yes" or "No" in column under Q. 10 below.*

11. Was anyone (else) in your family or household injured seriously enough to be treated medically? *Enter "Yes" or "No" in column under Q. 11 below.*

12. Please estimate the total dollar amount of flood damage. *Enter dollar damage in column under Q. 12 below.*

Repeat Q. 9, 10, 11, and 12 for all other years in which floods occurred.

Q. 8 Year	Q. 9 No. Floods	Q. 10 Killed Yes	No	Q. 11 Injured Yes	No	Q. 12 $ Damage
1970( )	_____	( )	( )	( )	( )	_____
1971( )	_____	( )	( )	( )	( )	_____
1972( )	_____	( )	( )	( )	( )	_____
1973( )	_____	( )	( )	( )	( )	_____
1974( )	_____	( )	( )	( )	( )	_____
1975( )	_____	( )	( )	( )	( )	_____
1976( )	_____	( )	( )	( )	( )	_____
1977( )	_____	( )	( )	( )	( )	_____
1978( )	_____	( )	( )	( )	( )	_____
1979( )	_____	( )	( )	( )	( )	_____
1980( )	_____	( )	( )	( )	( )	_____

13. Since 1970, has your family or household experienced a hurricane or severe tropical storm in a house or apartment in which you were living as a group?   **Yes** ( )   **Ask Q. 14**   **No** ( )   **Skip to Q. 19**

If "Yes" in Q. 13, Ask:

14. In which year or years did the hurricane or hurricanes, storm or storms occur? *Check all years that apply in column under Q. 14 below.*

For Each Year Checked in Q. 14, Ask:

15. Now, thinking about (*insert first year mentioned in Q. 14*) how many hurricanes or tropical storms did your family or household experience during that year? *Enter number of hurricanes/storms in column under Q. 15 below.*

16. Was anyone in your family or household killed as a result of injuries due to hurricane or storm? *Enter "Yes" or "No" in column under Q. 16 below.*

17. Was anyone (else) in your family or household injured seriously enough to be treated medically? *Enter "Yes" or "No" in column under Q. 17 below.*

18. Please estimate the total dollar amount of hurricane or storm damage. *Enter dollar damage in column under Q. 18 below.*

Repeat Q. 15, 16, 17, and 18 for all years in which hurricanes/storms occurred.

Q. 14 Year	Q. 15 Hurricanes/Storms	Q. 16 Killed Yes	No	Q. 17 Injured Yes	No	Q. 18 $ Damage
1970( )	_____	( )	( )	( )	( )	_____
1971( )	_____	( )	( )	( )	( )	_____
1972( )	_____	( )	( )	( )	( )	_____
1973( )	_____	( )	( )	( )	( )	_____
1974( )	_____	( )	( )	( )	( )	_____
1975( )	_____	( )	( )	( )	( )	_____
1976( )	_____	( )	( )	( )	( )	_____
1977( )	_____	( )	( )	( )	( )	_____
1978( )	_____	( )	( )	( )	( )	_____
1979( )	_____	( )	( )	( )	( )	_____
1980( )	_____	( )	( )	( )	( )	_____

19. Since 1970, has your family or household experienced a tornado or severe windstorm in a house or apartment in which you were living as a group?   **Yes ( ) Ask Q. 20**
No ( ) Skip to Q. 25

If "Yes" in Q. 19, Ask:

20. In which year or years did the tornado or tornadoes, windstorm or windstorms occur? *Check all years that apply in column under Q. 20 below.*

    For Each Year Checked in Q. 20, Ask:

    21. Now, thinking about (*insert first year mentioned in Q. 20*) how many tornadoes or windstorms did your family or household experience during that year? *Enter number of tornadoes/windstorms in column under Q. 21 below.*

    22. Was anyone in your family or household killed as a result of injuries due to tornado or windstorm? *Enter "Yes" or "No" in column under Q. 22 below.*

    23. Was anyone (else) in your family or household injured seriously enough to be treated medically? *Enter "Yes" or "No" in column under Q. 23 below.*

    24. Please estimate the total dollar amount of tornado or windstorm damage. *Enter dollar damage in column under Q. 24 below.*

    Repeat Q. 21, 22, 23, and 24 for all other years in which tornadoes or windstorms occurred.

Q. 20 Year	Q. 21 Tornadoes/Windstorms	Q. 22 Killed Yes No	Q. 23 Injured Yes No	Q. 24 $ Damage
1970( )	_____	( ) ( )	( ) ( )	_____
1971( )	_____	( ) ( )	( ) ( )	_____
1972( )	_____	( ) ( )	( ) ( )	_____
1973( )	_____	( ) ( )	( ) ( )	_____
1974( )	_____	( ) ( )	( ) ( )	_____
1975( )	_____	( ) ( )	( ) ( )	_____

```
1976( ) _____  ( ) ( ) ( ) ( ) _____
1977( ) _____  ( ) ( ) ( ) ( ) _____
1978( ) _____  ( ) ( ) ( ) ( ) _____
1979( ) _____  ( ) ( ) ( ) ( ) _____
1980( ) _____  ( ) ( ) ( ) ( ) _____
```

25. Since 1970, has your family or household experienced an earthquake or tremor in a house or apartment in which you were living as a group?

    Yes ( )   **Ask Q. 26**
    No ( ) **Skip to Q. 31**

If "Yes" in Q. 25, Ask:

26. In which year or years did the earthquake or quakes, tremor or tremors occur? *Check all years that apply in column under Q. 26 below.*

   For Each Year Checked in Q. 26, Ask:

   27. Now, thinking about (*insert first year mentioned in Q. 26*) how many earthquakes or tremors did your family or household experience during that year? *Enter number of earthquakes/ tremors in column under Q. 27 below.*

   28. Was anyone in your family or household killed as a result of injuries due to earthquake or tremor? *Enter "Yes" or "No" in column under Q. 28 below.*

   29. Was anyone (else) in your family or household injured seriously enough to be treated medically? *Enter "Yes" or "No" in column under Q. 29 below.*

   30. Please estimate the total dollar amount of earthquake or tremor damage. *Enter dollar damage in column under Q. 30 below.*

   Repeat Q. 27, 28, 29, and 30 for all other years in which earthquakes or tremors occurred.

Q. 26 Year	Q. 27 No. Quakes/Tremors	Q. 28 Killed		Q. 29 Injured		Q. 30 $ Damage
		Yes	No	Yes	No	
1970( )	_____	( )	( )	( )	( )	_____
1971( )	_____	( )	( )	( )	( )	_____
1972( )	_____	( )	( )	( )	( )	_____
1973( )	_____	( )	( )	( )	( )	_____
1974( )	_____	( )	( )	( )	( )	_____
1975( )	_____	( )	( )	( )	( )	_____
1976( )	_____	( )	( )	( )	( )	_____
1977( )	_____	( )	( )	( )	( )	_____
1978( )	_____	( )	( )	( )	( )	_____
1979( )	_____	( )	( )	( )	( )	_____
1980( )	_____	( )	( )	( )	( )	_____

Ask Everyone:

31. In order to present our findings separately for different kinds of families, it is important that we obtain some additional information.

   How many persons over 16 years of age are living in your household?   _____

32. How many persons 16 years of age or younger are living in your household?   _____

33. What is the age of the main wage-earner in the household?   _____

34. Do you own or rent your house or apartment?   _____

35. How would you describe the community in which you are living?

   ( ) Rural area
   ( ) Small town under 25,000 population
   ( ) Suburban residential area of a city over 25,000 population
   ( ) Medium-sized city with a population between 25,000 and 250,000
   ( ) Large city over 250,000 population

36. In what year was your household started? That is, when did you begin living together as a family?   _____ Year

37. In 1979, was your total   **Above $12,000** ( )   **Ask Q. 38**
household income above or   **Below $12,000** ( )   **Skip to Q. 41**
below $12,000?

**If Above $12,000 in Q. 37,
Ask:**

     38. Was your total house-   **Above $15,000** ( )   **Ask Q. 39**
         hold income above or   **Below $15,000** ( )   **Skip to Q. 42**
         below $15,000?

         **If Above $15,000 in
         Q. 38, Ask:**

             39. Was your total   **Above $20,000** ( )   **Ask Q. 40**
                 household income   **Below $20,000** ( )   **Skip to Q. 42**
                 above or below
                 $20,000?

                 **If Above $20,000
                 in Q. 39, Ask:**

                     40. Was your total   **Above $30,000** ( )
                         household   **Below $30,000** ( )   **Skip to Q. 42**
                         income above
                         or below
                         $30,000?

   **If "Below $12,000" in
   Q. 37, Ask:**

     41. Was your total house-   **Above $6,000** ( )
         hold income above or   **Below $6,000** ( )
         below $6,000?

Ask Everyone:

42. What is the race of persons living in the house-   White   ( )
     hold? Are they . . . *read list.*   Black   ( )
                                                     Other   ( )

43. Sex of respondent. *Do not read.*   Male   ( )
                                                          Female   ( )

If "Yes" to Q. 1, 7, 13, 19, or 25, Ask:

44. We are interested in learning more about your household's experi-
    ences with natural disasters—kinds of damage, injuries, insurance
    experience, and so on. We will send you a short questionnaire to
    complete, and for this, we need the name and address of someone
    in your family who has such information.

    Name _____

    Street Address _____

    Town or City _____

    State _____ **Zip** _____

Programmer: Insert "Thank you very much for your cooperation"
for households not requiring Q. 45–61.

**Special Instructions for Programmer: The following questions (45–61)
are to be asked in every tenth household.**

Now I will read a list of acts of nature or other serious events that sometimes
happen to people. For each event, please tell me whether your family or
household has had any experiences of that sort since 1970. Let's start with
"lightning strikes." *If the answer to an event is "yes," ask immediately
whether there were damages or injuries.*

	Happened		Damages/ Injuries	
	No	Yes	No	Yes
45. Lightning strikes	( )	( )	( )	( )
46. Landslides or cave-ins	( )	( )	( )	( )
47. Severe hailstorms	( )	( )	( )	( )
48. Serious auto accident	( )	( )	( )	( )

49. Victim of burglary, robbery, or assault	( )	( )	( )	( )
50. Arrest or imprisonment	( )	( )	( )	( )
51. Severe snowstorms	( )	( )	( )	( )
52. Ground around house subsiding	( )	( )	( )	( )
53. Drug or alcohol addiction	( )	( )	( )	( )
54. Victim of shooting	( )	( )	( )	( )

Has your family or household experienced any of the following events since 1970?

	Happened	
	No	Yes
55. Being unemployed and seeking employment for over six months	( )	( )
56. Personal bankruptcy	( )	( )
57. Severe mental depression	( )	( )
58. Children having trouble in school	( )	( )
59. Unexpected death of household member	( )	( )
60. Marital breakup	( )	( )
61. Birth of defective child	( )	( )

Thank you very much for your cooperation.

Call Record Form for Disaster Victimization Screener

Initial Disposition	First Call	Second Callback	Callback
1. Nonworking/wrong number	( )	( )	( )
2. No answer/busy (*callback*)	( )	( )	( )

3. Household head refused interview   ( )   ( )   ( )
4. Household head terminated interview   ( )   ( )   ( )
5. Household head not available   ( )   ( )   ( )
   (*make appointment for callback*)
6. Other (*specify*)   ( )   ( )   ( )

_____

To make appointment for callback, say:

When would it be convenient for me to call back and speak with you (him/her)? *Record day, date, and time for callback.*

	Day	Date	Time
1.	_____	_____	_____
2.	_____	_____	_____
3.	_____	_____	_____

NATIONAL STUDY
OF HOUSEHOLD EXPERIENCES
WITH ACTS OF NATURE AND
HOUSEHOLD FIRES

PETER H. ROSSI
JAMES D. WRIGHT

Social and Demographic Research Institute
University of Massachusetts
Amherst, Massachusetts 01003

CONDUCTED BY:

AUDITS & SURVEYS, INC.
One Park Avenue
New York, New York 10016

WHAT IS THIS SURVEY ABOUT?

- Your family's or household group's EXPERIENCES WITH DAMAGES AND INJURIES FROM SUCH HAZARDS AS A HURRICANE OR TROPICAL STORM during the last decade (1970-1980).
- We are especially concerned with THE COSTS AND FINANCIAL IMPACTS ON YOUR FAMILY OR HOUSEHOLD GROUP.

WHAT WILL BE DONE WITH THE INFORMATION?

- Summaries of your experiences and those of other families will be put together in a report that will be presented to CONGRESS, FEDERAL, STATE AND LOCAL AGENCIES that are responsible for programs designed to help the victims of fires and natural hazards.
- NO INFORMATION YOU GIVE US WILL BE REVEALED TO ANYONE IN A WAY THAT CAN IDENTIFY YOU OR YOUR FAMILY OR HOUSEHOLD GROUP.

HOW WERE YOU CHOSEN TO FILL OUT THIS QUESTIONNAIRE?

- We telephoned a representative sample of private, residential telephone numbers in the continental United States. YOUR NUMBER WAS PICKED BY CHANCE.
- When we called, someone in your household (perhaps yourself) told us that during the period 1970 to 1980, a hurricane or tropical storm injured someone in your household or damaged your property or personal possessions. Our interviewer said we were interested in learning more about your family's or household's experience with such hazards and your name was given as a knowledgeable person who could complete a short question- naire on injuries or damages.

WHAT IF YOU HAVE RECEIVED MORE THAN ONE QUESTIONNAIRE?

- This means that the person we spoke to in your family or household reported several hazard events. For example, if you had a fire in 1971 and a flood in 1978, you have received two questionnaires. Please complete a separate questionnaire for each hazard event. The type of hazard and year it happened is printed at the top of the first page of the questionnaire.

HOW TO FILL OUT THE QUESTIONNAIRE.

- Most of the questions can be answered by circling a number that corresponds to your answer, as follows:

    What is your marital status?

    1   Married

    ② Single and never married

    3   Married but separated

    4   Widowed or divorced

PLEASE ANSWER EVERY QUESTION THAT APPLIES TO YOUR EXPERIENCES.

IF YOU HAVE ANY QUESTIONS ABOUT THE SURVEY CALL DR. ROSSI OR DR. WRIGHT COLLECT 413-545-3418.

B-13

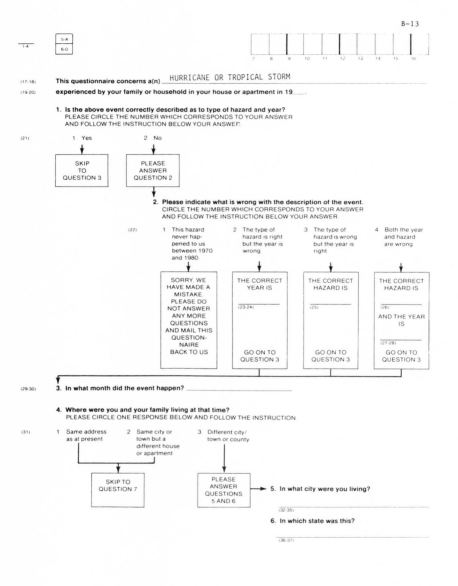

1-4

5-A
6-0

(17-18) This questionnaire concerns a(n) ___HURRICANE OR TROPICAL STORM___

(19-20) experienced by your family or household in your house or apartment in 19___.

1. Is the above event correctly described as to type of hazard and year?
    PLEASE CIRCLE THE NUMBER WHICH CORRESPONDS TO YOUR ANSWER
    AND FOLLOW THE INSTRUCTION BELOW YOUR ANSWER.

(21)   1   Yes   2   No

         SKIP   PLEASE
         TO   ANSWER
         QUESTION 3   QUESTION 2

2. Please indicate what is wrong with the description of the event.
    CIRCLE THE NUMBER WHICH CORRESPONDS TO YOUR ANSWER
    AND FOLLOW THE INSTRUCTION BELOW YOUR ANSWER.

(22)   1   This hazard   2   The type of   3   The type of   4   Both the year
            never hap-   hazard is right   hazard is wrong   and hazard
            pened to us   but the year is   but the year is   are wrong
            between 1970   wrong   right
            and 1980

        SORRY, WE   THE CORRECT   THE CORRECT   THE CORRECT
        HAVE MADE A   YEAR IS   HAZARD IS   HAZARD IS
        MISTAKE.
        PLEASE DO   (23-24)   (25)   (26)
        NOT ANSWER
        ANY MORE   AND THE YEAR
        QUESTIONS   IS
        AND MAIL THIS
        QUESTION-   (27-28)
        NAIRE
        BACK TO US   GO ON TO   GO ON TO   GO ON TO
                           QUESTION 3   QUESTION 3   QUESTION 3

(29-30) 3. In what month did the event happen? _____

4. Where were you and your family living at that time?
    PLEASE CIRCLE ONE RESPONSE BELOW AND FOLLOW THE INSTRUCTION

(31)   1   Same address   2   Same city or   3   Different city/
           as at present   town but a   town or county
                                different house
                                or apartment

                    SKIP TO   PLEASE
                    QUESTION 7   ANSWER   →   5. In what city were you living?
                                            QUESTIONS
                                            5 AND 6   (32-35)

                                                             6. In which state was this?

                                                                (36-37)

7. Before the hazard event happened, did you have any warning that the event was going to happen?

(38)

1   Yes   2   No

| PLEASE ANSWER | SKIP TO |
| QUESTIONS 8 AND 9 | QUESTION 10 |

8. What kind or kinds of warning(s) did you get?
PLEASE CIRCLE "YES" OR "NO" TO EACH TYPE OF WARNING.

	Yes	No	
(39)	1	2	Weather or news reports on radio or TV
(40)	1	2	Neighbors
(41)	1	2	Friend or relative
(42)	1	2	Smoke detection or some other device in the home
(43)	1	2	Siren
(44)	1	2	Police, civil defense or firemen coming to the house
(45)	1	2	Some other way — PLEASE DESCRIBE

(46-47)

9. What did you and your family or household do in response to the warning?
PLEASE CIRCLE "YES" OR "NO" TO EACH TYPE OF RESPONSE.

	Yes	No	
(48)	1	2	Nothing, thought it was a false alarm
(49)	1	2	Nothing, did not know what to do
(50)	1	2	Nothing, thought it did not apply to us
(51)	1	2	Nothing, but tried to get more information
(52)	1	2	Nothing, did not think the coming event would be serious enough to do anything about it
(53)	1	2	Left the house as quickly as we could
(54)	1	2	Tried to find a safe place in the house
(55)	1	2	We did something else: PLEASE DESCRIBE

(56-57)

10. Was anyone in your family or household injured or killed or did anyone become physically sick as a result of the event?

(58)

1   Yes   2   No

| PLEASE ANSWER | SKIP TO |
| QUESTIONS 11 AND 12 | QUESTION 13 |

11. How many people were injured, killed or became physically sick?

(59-60)

GO ON TO QUESTION 12 ON THE NEXT PAGE

12. **For each person injured, killed or made physically sick, please answer the following questions in the grid below.**
WE HAVE PROVIDED SPACE FOR FOUR (4) PERSONS. IF THE NUMBER WAS GREATER THAN FOUR, INCLUDE ONLY THE MOST SERIOUS CASES.
PLEASE ANSWER EACH QUESTION FOR EACH PERSON

	PERSON A	PERSON B	PERSON C	PERSON D
Age WRITE AGE IN HERE →	_____ YEARS (61-62)	5-B 6-C _____ YEARS (7-8)	_____ YEARS (23-24)	_____ YEARS (39-40)
Sex				
Male	1	1	1	1
Female	2 (63)	2 (9)	2 (25)	2 (41)
Result?				
Injured	1	1	1	1
Killed	2	2	2	2
Physically ill	3 (64)	3 (10)	3 (26)	3 (42)
Treated by Doctor?				
Yes	1	1	1	1
No	2 (65)	2 (11)	2 (27)	2 (43)
Hospitalized?				
Yes	1	1	1	1
No	2 (66)	2 (12)	2 (28)	2 (44)
Unable to Work or go to School for Any Period?				
Yes	1	1	1	1
No	2 (67)	2 (13)	2 (29)	2 (45)
Injury Still Bother Person Now?				
Yes	1	1	1	1
No	2 (68)	2 (14)	2 (30)	2 (46)
Cost of Medical Care (Doctors, Hospital, Medicine) Before Insurance?	$_____ (69-74)	$_____ (15-20)	$_____ (31-36)	$_____ (47-52)
Insurance Paid Any of the Cost?				
Yes	1	1	1	1
No	2 (75)	2 (21)	2 (37)	2 (53)
Anyone Else Pay for the Medical Care?				
Yes	1	1	1	1
No	2 (76)	2 (22)	2 (38)	2 (54)

13. **Did you and your family or household suffer any damage to your house or apartment or damages to your furniture or personal property as a result of the event?**

(55)

1 Yes   2 No

| PLEASE ANSWER QUESTION 14 | SKIP TO QUESTION 15 |

14. **What kind of damage or damages did you suffer?**
PLEASE CIRCLE "NO" OR "YES" FOR EACH KIND OF DAMAGE IN THE LIST BELOW.
IF YOU ANSWER "YES," FILL IN THE AMOUNT OF DAMAGE.
USE YOUR BEST ESTIMATE IF YOU DON'T REMEMBER THE EXACT AMOUNT.

	DAMAGED? No	Yes	AMOUNT OF DAMAGE	
Roof on building?	2	1 →	$	(56. 57-62)
Basement or foundation?	2	1 →	$	(63. 64-69)
Walls or floors?	2	1 →	$	(70. 71-76)
Windows or doors?	2	1 →	$	5-C 6-0 (7. 8-13)
Yard and landscaping?	2	1 →	$	(14. 15-20)
Garage or other building on property?	2	1 →	$	(21. 22-27)
Furnace, air conditioner or hot water heater?	2	1 →	$	(28. 29-34)
Other part of building?	2	1 →	$	(35. 36-41)
Furniture?	2	1 →	$	(42. 43-48)
Clothes?	2	1 →	$	(49. 50-55)
Rugs or curtains?	2	1 →	$	(56. 57-62)
Appliances (stoves, refrigerators, washing machines, etc.)?	2	1 →	$	5-D 6-0 (7. 8-13)
Books or papers?	2	1 →	$	(14. 15-20)
Pets?	2	1 →	$	(21. 22-27)
Radio, TV or stereo?	2	1 →	$	(28. 29-34)
Jewelry?	2	1 →	$	(35. 36-41)
Cars, trucks or other vehicles?	2	1 →	$	(42. 43-48)
Any other personal property?	2	1 →	$	(49. 50-55)

15. Did you lose any things that were especially valuable because of their sentimental associations and that would be difficult or impossible to replace?

(56)

1 Yes   2 No

PLEASE ANSWER   SKIP TO
QUESTION 16   QUESTION 17

16. Please indicate the kinds of things you lost.
CIRCLE AS MANY AS APPLY.

(57)	1	Jewelry or personal clothing with sentimental value
(58)	1	Important documents such as diplomas, passports, birth certificates, etc.
(59)	1	Letters and photographs
(60)	1	Heirlooms, antiques and one-of-a-kind furniture
(61)	1	Something else that was irreplaceable PLEASE DESCRIBE

(62-63)

17. Did you have to leave your house or apartment either before or after the event for any period of time?

(64)

1 Yes, before the   2 Yes, after the   3 No
   event to avoid   event because of
   injuries   damages or
                              injuries

PLEASE ANSWER   PLEASE ANSWER   SKIP TO
QUESTIONS   QUESTIONS   QUESTION
18 AND 19   18 AND 19   20

(65-67)

18. How long did you have to live somewhere else — how many days? _____

19. Where did you stay?
PLEASE ANSWER "YES" OR "NO" TO EACH TYPE OF PLACE.

	Yes	No	
(68)	1	2	Emergency shelter provided by community or by disaster services
(69)	1	2	Motel or hotel
(70)	1	2	With friends
(71)	1	2	With relatives
(72)	1	2	Someplace else

220 APPENDIX B-1

20. What were the total dollar costs to you and your family that resulted from the event?
PLEASE INCLUDE THE COSTS THAT RESULTED FROM THE INJURIES AND DAMAGES YOU LISTED IN QUESTIONS 12 AND 14, ANY LOSSES OF VALUABLES IN QUESTION 16, COSTS OF LIVING IN OTHER PLACES IN QUESTION 18 AND ANY OTHER EXPENSES YOU HAD AS A RESULT OF THE EVENT.

INCLUDE ALL COSTS EVEN IF THEY WERE PAID BY SOMEONE ELSE.

PLEASE ESTIMATE IF YOU CAN'T RECALL EXACT COSTS.

DO NOT INCLUDE DAMAGES TO FARM BUILDINGS, CROPS OR TO BUSINESSES OR ANY OTHER INCOME PRODUCING PROPERTY.

JUST INCLUDE THE DAMAGES TO YOUR HOME, APARTMENT OR HOUSE AND PERSONAL PROPERTY.

(73-78)   **Total dollar cost:** $_____

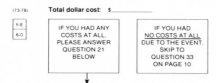

5-E
6-0

IF YOU HAD ANY COSTS AT ALL, PLEASE ANSWER QUESTION 21 BELOW

IF YOU HAD NO COSTS AT ALL DUE TO THE EVENT, SKIP TO QUESTION 33 ON PAGE 10

21. At the time the event occurred, did you have any insurance on your property or personal possessions that you thought would cover any of the losses and expenses connected with the event?

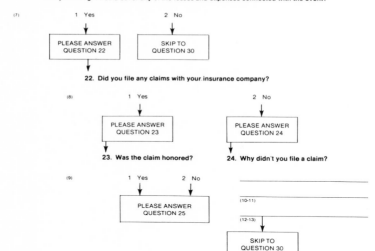

(7)   1 Yes   2 No

PLEASE ANSWER QUESTION 22

SKIP TO QUESTION 30

22. Did you file any claims with your insurance company?

(8)   1 Yes   2 No

PLEASE ANSWER QUESTION 23

PLEASE ANSWER QUESTION 24

23. Was the claim honored?   **24. Why didn't you file a claim?**

(9)   1 Yes   2 No   _____

PLEASE ANSWER QUESTION 25

(10-11) _____

(12-13)

SKIP TO QUESTION 30

IF YOU FILED A CLAIM PLEASE ANSWER QUESTION 25. BELOW

25. On the whole, how fairly do you think the insurance company treated your claim?
PLEASE CIRCLE THE ONE NUMBER THAT CORRESPONDS WITH YOUR ANSWER

(14)

1 Very fair treatment	2 Somewhat fair treatment	3 Somewhat unfair treatment	4 Very unfair treatment

SKIP TO
QUESTION 27

PLEASE ANSWER
QUESTION 26

**26. Did your insurance company do any
of the following things?**
PLEASE ANSWER "YES" OR "NO" TO EACH ITEM

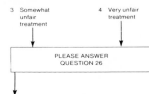

	Yes	No	
(15)	1	2	Process your claim too slowly
(16)	1	2	Disallow claim unfairly
(17)	1	2	Did not pay enough to replace damaged or lost property
(18)	1	2	Company representative was bad mannered
(19)	1	2	Company did something else that was unfair

27. Did you receive any payments on your claim from your insurance company?

(20)

1 Yes   2 No

| PLEASE ANSWER QUESTIONS 28 AND 29 | SKIP TO QUESTION 30 |

28. How much of the costs of replacing or repairing damaged property did the insurance company pay?
CIRCLE ONLY ONE ANSWER BELOW.

(21)

1 None

2 Less than 10%

3 10% — 29%

4 30% — 49%

5 50% — 69%

6 70% — 89%

7 90% — 100%

29. For what damages did you receive payment from your insurance company?
PLEASE CIRCLE "NO" OR "YES" TO EACH KIND OF DAMAGE LISTED.
FOR EACH KIND OF DAMAGE FOR WHICH YOU RECEIVED PAYMENT,
INDICATE THE AMOUNT OF MONEY YOU WERE REIMBURSED.
PLEASE ESTIMATE IF YOU DO NOT KNOW THE EXACT AMOUNT.

	RECEIVED PAYMENT?		AMOUNT REIMBURSED BY INSURANCE	
	No	Yes		
Damage to building you lived in	2	1 ⟶	$ _____	(22, 23-28)
Costs of injuries received by persons	2	1 ⟶	$ _____	(29, 30-35)
Damage to personal possessions (clothes, furniture, etc.)	2	1 ⟶	$ _____	(36, 37-42)
Damage to cars or trucks	2	1 ⟶	$ _____	(43, 44-49)
Other damage	2	1 ⟶	$ _____	(50, 51-56)

IF YOU HAD ANY COSTS OR EXPENSES DUE TO THE EVENT, ANSWER QUESTION 30.

30. **Did you receive any help in paying these expenses from any of the following sources?**
PLEASE CHECK "NO" OR "YES" TO EACH SOURCE.
IF YOU RECEIVED MONEY, PLEASE INDICATE THE AMOUNT.
IF THE HELP WAS IN THE FORM OF A LOAN, ENTER THE AMOUNT IN THE "LOAN" COLUMN BELOW.
IF A GRANT OR GIFT, USE THE GIFT COLUMN.

| | RECEIVED FINANCIAL HELP? | | AMOUNT RECEIVED | | |
	No	Yes	As Loan	As Grant or Gift	
American Red Cross	2	1 →	$	$	(7, 8-19) 5-F 6-0
Relatives	2	1 →	$	$	(20, 21, 32)
Small Business Administration business loan	2	1 →	$	$	(33, 34-45)
Small Business Administration personal loan	2	1 →	$	$	(46, 47-58)
Farmers Home Administration	2	1 →	$	$	(59, 60-71)
FDAA (Federal Disaster Assistance Administration)	2	1 →	$	$	(7, 8-19) 5-G 6-0
FEMA (Federal Emergency Management Agency)	2	1 →	$	$	(20, 21-32)
Veterans' Administration	2	1 →	$	$	(33, 34-45)
Unemployment insurance	2	1 →	$	$	(46, 47-58)
Other federal government agency or program	2	1 →	$	$	(59, 60-71)
Local bank or savings and loan	2	1 →	$	$	(7, 8-19) 5-H 6-0
Local community organization	2	1 →	$	$	(20, 21-32)
Church or Synagogue	2	1 →	$	$	(33, 34-45)
State government agency	2	1 →	$	$	(46, 47-58)
Local government agency	2	1 →	$	$	(59, 60-71)
Labor union	2	1 →	$	$	(7, 8-19) 5-I 6-0
Employer	2	1 →	$	$	(20, 21-32)
Some other help (DESCRIBE)	2	1 →	$	$	(33, 34-45)
					(46-47)

31. Did you take a deduction from your income tax for the expenses you had in connection with the event?

(48)

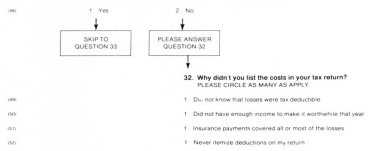

1 Yes   2 No

SKIP TO   PLEASE ANSWER
QUESTION 33   QUESTION 32

32. Why didn't you list the costs in your tax return?
PLEASE CIRCLE AS MANY AS APPLY

(49)   1   Did not know that losses were tax deductible

(50)   1   Did not have enough income to make it worthwhile that year

(51)   1   Insurance payments covered all or most of the losses

(52)   1   Never itemize deductions on my return

33. Was there any interruption in public utilities at your home or in your immediate neighborhood because of the event?
PLEASE CIRCLE "NO" OR "YES" TO EACH UTILITY LISTED BELOW.
IF "YES," ENTER THE NUMBER OF DAYS THE UTILITY WAS INTERRUPTED.

	INTERRUPTED?		NUMBER OF DAYS INTERRUPTED	
	No	Yes		
Gas	2	1 →		(53 54-56)
Electricity	2	1 →		(57 58-60)
Water	2	1 →		(61 62-64)
Sewer	2	1 →		(65 66-68)
Garbage Collection	2	1 →		(69 70-72)
Public Transportation	2	1 →		(73 74-76)
Telephone Service	2	1 →		(77 78-80)

34. As a result of the event, were any other homes or apartments damaged on your block or in your neighborhood?
CIRCLE "NO" OR "YES" TO EACH AREA BELOW.
IF "YES," ENTER THE NUMBER OF HOMES DAMAGED — ESTIMATE IF YOU ARE UNSURE.

	OTHER HOMES OR APARTMENTS DAMAGED?		NUMBER OF OTHER HOMES OR APARTMENTS DAMAGED	
	No	Yes		
Your block	2	1 →		(7 8-13) 5-J / 6-0
Your neighborhood	2	1 →		(14 15-20)
Your city or town	2	1 →		(21 22-27)

35. Several private groups and government agencies offer help to victims of disasters and fires.
In connection with this event, did any of the following agencies contact you or did you contact them?

PLEASE CIRCLE "NO," "NOT SURE" OR "YES" TO EACH GROUP OR AGENCY CONTACTED.

FOR EACH AGENCY WITH WHICH YOU HAD CONTACT, CIRCLE YOUR DEGREE OF SATISFACTION
WITH THE CONTACT — "HIGH," "MEDIUM" OR "LOW."

CIRCLE "NO" OR "YES" AS TO WHETHER YOU RECEIVED ANY ACTUAL HELP FROM THE CONTACTED AGENCY.

	WERE YOU CONTACTED?			SATISFACTION WITH CONTACT?			RECEIVE ANY HELP?		
	No	Not Sure	Yes	High	Medium	Low	Yes	No	
Fire Department	2	3	1	1	2	3	1	2	(28, 29-30)
Local, County, Sheriff or State Police Department	2	3	1	1	2	3	1	2	(31, 32-33)
American Red Cross	2	3	1	1	2	3	1	2	(34, 35-36)
National Guard	2	3	1	1	2	3	1	2	(37, 38-39)
Salvation Army	2	3	1	1	2	3	1	2	(40, 41-42)
Local church or synagogue	2	3	1	1	2	3	1	2	(43, 44-45)
Federal Disaster Assistance Agency (FDAA)	2	3	1	1	2	3	1	2	(46, 47-48)
Local welfare department	2	3	1	1	2	3	1	2	(49, 50-51)
Small Business Administration	2	3	1	1	2	3	1	2	(52, 53-54)
Farmers Home Administration (FHA)	2	3	1	1	2	3	1	2	(55, 56-57)
Civil Defense	2	3	1	1	2	3	1	2	(58, 59-60)
Federal Emergency Management Administration (FEMA)	2	3	1	1	2	3	1	2	(61, 62-63)
Labor union	2	3	1	1	2	3	1	2	(64, 65-66)
Veterans' Administration	2	3	1	1	2	3	1	2	(67, 68-69)
Military units of the Regular Army	2	3	1	1	2	3	1	2	(70, 71-72)
Local hospital	2	3	1	1	2	3	1	2	(73, 74-75)
Local civic organizations (e.g., Lions, Kiwanis, Chamber of Commerce, etc.)	2	3	1	1	2	3	1	2	(7, 8-9) 5-K 6-0
Mennonite Relief Organization	2	3	1	1	2	3	1	2	(10, 11-12)
Local public works department	2	3	1	1	2	3	1	2	(13, 14-15)

36. Did you get any help from friends or relatives?
PLEASE CIRCLE "NO" OR "YES" TO EACH SOURCE OF HELP.
IF "YES" TO HELP, CIRCLE THE KIND OR KINDS OF HELP RECEIVED.

	RECEIVED HELP?			KIND OF HELP (CIRCLE AS MANY AS APPLY)				
	No	Yes		Shelter	Loans	Gifts	Labor	
Friends	2	1	→	1	1	1	1	(16, 17-20)
Relatives	2	1	→	1	1	1	1	(21, 22-25)
Neighbors	2	1	→	1	1	1	1	(26, 27-30)
Church or Synagogue	2	1	→	1	1	1	1	(31, 32-35)
Co-workers	2	1	→	1	1	1	1	(36, 37-40)
Employer	2	1	→	1	1	1	1	(41, 42-45)

**37. How long did it take you to fix up your house and
get repairs done to be as comfortable as you were before the event?**

(46)

1   Damage too much to repair

2   No time at all because little or no damage

3   At least a few days to repair

(47-49)   **38. How many days?** _____

(50-52)   **39. All told, how long did it take for you and
your family to settle back into
your routine, after the event — how many days?** _____

40. As a result of the event, did any of the following happen to you or your family?
PLEASE CIRCLE "NO" OR "YES" TO EACH ITEM.

	No	Yes	
(53)	2	1	Went into debt borrowing money to pay for medical bills
(54)	2	1	Went into debt to pay bills for repairs to property or replacement of things destroyed
(55)	2	1	Was unemployed for more than a week because of damage to the place where you worked
(56)	2	1	Became depressed over the event
(57)	2	1	Decided to move because it was too dangerous living in that location
(58)	2	1	Looked into getting more insurance coverage for events of that sort
(59)	2	1	Had to use up our savings to pay for losses and expenses
(60)	2	1	Had to sell some of our things to pay for losses and expenses
(61)	2	1	Had to get an additional mortgage (or bigger mortgage) to finance repairs to my house
(62)	2	1	Went into debt so deeply to pay for damages and/or injuries that we had to go without a lot of necessities to pay back our debts

41. At the time the event occurred, did you own or rent your house or apartment?

(63)

1 Rent   2 Own
   ↓   ↓

41a. What was your monthly rental,   **41b. What was the approximate value of your home**
excluding utilities?   — what price do you think you could have sold
                                                it for at at the time?

$ _____ $ _____
(64-69)   (70-75)

FAMILY BACKGROUND QUESTIONS

42. What is the make-up of your household?
PLEASE ENTER BELOW THE RELATIONSHIP TO YOU AND THE AGE OF EACH PERSON LIVING IN YOUR HOUSEHOLD USING CIRCLES. INDICATE THE SEX OF ALL PERSONS, WHETHER OR NOT THEY ARE EMPLOYED AND WHETHER OR NOT THEY WERE LIVING WITH YOU AT THE TIME OF THE EVENT.
START WITH YOURSELF ON THE FIRST LINE.

5-L
6-0

RELATIONSHIP TO YOU	AGE	SEX MALE	SEX FEMALE	EMPLOYED? Yes	EMPLOYED? No	LIVED IN HOUSEHOLD AT TIME OF EVENT? Yes	LIVED IN HOUSEHOLD AT TIME OF EVENT? No	
YOURSELF	___	1	2	1	2	1	2	(7-11)
	___	1	2	1	2	1	2	(12-16)
	___	1	2	1	2	1	2	(17-21)
	___	1	2	1	2	1	2	(22-26)
	___	1	2	1	2	1	2	(27-31)
	___	1	2	1	2	1	2	(32-36)
	___	1	2	1	2	1	2	(37-41)
	___	1	2	1	2	1	2	(42-46)

43. How much formal education have you had?
PLEASE CIRCLE ONLY ONE ANSWER BELOW.

1 Did not graduate from high school (47)

2 High school graduate

3 Some college

4 College graduate

5 Graduate or professional training beyond college graduate

44. Do you own or rent the house or apartment you are living in now?

1 Own (48)

2 Rent

45. Do you have any of the following kinds of insurance coverage at the present time?
PLEASE CIRCLE "YES" OR "NO" TO EACH KIND LISTED BELOW.

	Yes	No	Not Sure	
(49)	1	2	3	Automobile liability
(50)	1	2	3	Fire insurance for house or apartment structure
(51)	1	2	3	Fire insurance on furniture and possessions
(52)	1	2	3	Flood insurance
(53)	1	2	3	Earthquake insurance
(54)	1	2	3	Windstorm insurance
(55)	1	2	3	Burglary insurance on furniture and possessions
(56)	1	2	3	Medical expenses insurance

46. What was your total family or household income in 1979 and what was it in the year you experienced the event?
CIRCLE THE APPROPRIATE NUMBER FOR 1979 AND THE YEAR OF THE EVENT.

	TOTAL FAMILY OR HOUSEHOLD INCOME	
	1979	Year of Event
Under $5,000	0	0
$5,000 to $7,499	1	1
$7,500 to $9,999	2	2
$10,000 to $12,499	3	3
$12,500 to $14,999	4	4
$15,000 to $19,999	5	5
$20,000 to $24,999	6	6
$25,000 to $29,999	7	7
$30,000 to $39,999	8	8
$40,000 or over	9	9

(57-58)

47. What is your family's racial background?
PLEASE CIRCLE ONLY ONE ANSWER BELOW.

(59)

1 White

2 Black

3 Hispanic

4 Oriental

5 American Indian

6 Other

B-28

48. Very often, when a hazard event occurs, other hazards are present, for example, an earthquake which causes a fire or a tropical storm which causes a flood.
PLEASE CIRCLE BELOW <u>EVERY</u> HAZARD THAT WAS PRESENT

(60)   1   Fire

(61)   1   Flood

(62)   1   Landslide

(63)   1   Hurricane

(64)   1   Tropical storm

(65)   1   Tornado

(66)   1   Windstorm

(67)   1   Earthquake

(68)   1   Lightning

THANK YOU VERY MUCH FOR ANSWERING THIS QUESTIONNAIRE.

PLEASE PLACE IT IN THE ADDRESSED, POSTAGE PAID ENVELOPE AND MAIL TO US.

FOR OFFICE USE ONLY

69	70	71	72	73	74	75	76	77	78

Index

231